BUS

Please renew or return items by the date
shown on your receipt

www.hertsdirect.org/libraries

Renewals and   0300 123 4049
enquiries:

Textphone for hearing   0300 123 4041
or speech impaired

D1375837

520 066 42 5

BEYOND FLYING

Rethinking air travel in a globally connected world

Edited by
CHRIS WATSON

green books

First published in 2014 by
Green Books
PO Box 145, Cambridge, CB4 1GQ, England
www.greenbooks.co.uk
+44 (0)1223 302 041

Green Books is an imprint of UIT Cambridge Ltd.

Preliminary editing by Whitireia Publishing
Front cover image courtesy of Wikimedia Commons

Cradle-to-cradle is a registered trademark of MBDC

Design by Jayne Jones

ISBN: 9780857842091 (paperback)
ISBN: 9780857842114 (ePub)
ISBN: 9780857842107 (PDF)
Also available for Kindle

Printed by CPI, England

Disclaimer: The advice herein is believed to be correct at
the time of printing, but the author and publisher accept
no liability for actions inspired by this book.

Email the editor at lessflying@gmail.com

10 9 8 7 6 5 4 3 2 1

Contents

Part 2 Savouring the journey

This book is dedicated to

Tony Gates
a man who knows human speed, and its value

Friends of the Earth: rethinking travel

Is flying a problem?

Flying has literally changed how we see the world. We can now visit places our grandparents only dreamed of. The social and cultural impacts of this have been, by and large, positive. Greater interaction has led to greater understanding and tolerance. Migration has led to more diverse communities. Far-flung communities have benefited from sharing new knowledge and greater connectedness with the rest of the globe.

But this freedom to fly has come at a cost for the environment. Aviation is a significant source of climate-changing gases and is rapidly growing in both developed and developing countries. And unlike most of our other activities – from heating our homes to travelling by car – planes can't as yet switch to non-fossil fuels.

Even in countries such as the UK, where there is significant opposition to the expansion of aviation, the industry continues to grow. The UK Department for Transport projects a doubling of passengers from 219 million in 2011 to 445 million by 2050.

This increase in flying is aided by financial subsidies, such as airlines not paying fuel tax or VAT on many parts of their operations. In the UK, this amounts to an effective subsidy from taxpayers of over £9 billion every year – that's more than £100 per person in the country.

But, if we are really serious about avoiding dangerous climate change, we have to recognize that fossil-fuel-powered aviation has to reduce its carbon emissions significantly. In practice, at least in the short to medium term, this means less flying, not more.

What's the solution?

Humans are a smart species. Although we do some stupid things, it's in our nature to look for solutions.

Friends of the Earth's starting point for solutions is research. We commissioned the UK's leading climate change research body, the Tyndall Centre, to report on the implications of aviation growth for policies designed to tackle climate change.

It concluded that the current rate of aviation growth would make it virtually impossible for the UK to meet its carbon dioxide (CO_2) reduction targets. The research said that we need a radical shift in UK and EU policy to bring emissions under control. Tyndall's findings form the basis for Friends of the Earth's position – that keeping a lid on aviation has to be part of the solution in addressing climate change.

The government and the aviation industry clearly must act. But, as consumers, we can also play a powerful role in reducing demand for flights.

Beyond Flying captures a new mindset and brings together numerous options for the open-minded traveller. It demonstrates that even the toughest of environmental challenges can be addressed.

There will be cases where flying is essential. For example, getting medicine to some remote communities might only be practical by air for some time to come. Perhaps one day we'll be able to power aeroplanes with fuels that are less polluting and that also don't conflict with food production or biodiversity protection.

But we're not there yet. And in the meantime we need practical solutions that help us travel or connect with each other without compromising the world our children will inherit. The trailblazers in *Beyond Flying* inspire us to do exactly that.

**Mike Childs, Head of Policy, Research and Science
Friends of the Earth**

Foreword
by Peter McManners

Photo © Peter McManners

The debate about the future of aviation in the face of climate change is highly polarised. On one side, aviation is the *bête noire* of the environmental movement; on the other, politicians and policymakers hold to the view that aviation is vital to the global economy. In the middle, the majority of people use cheap flights believing that there are few alternative realistic choices. There is a stalemate which must be broken. That can happen if two things occur. First, if people stop seeing the current unsustainable system of mass air travel as somehow inevitable, and understand that it actually rests on a few key policies that can be readily changed, and probably will be within the next decade. Second, if they are given practical alternatives.

Others, including myself, have written about the artificial incentives that prop up the current system, including the international rules which tax jet fuel less than the fuel in your car, as well as the lack of accounting for pollution from planes, such as soot and CO_2, that crosses international borders.

Beyond Flying is concerned with practical alternatives, which includes exploring attitudes to travel.

For people persuaded that climate change is an emergency, and that everyone should make changes in their travel plans to reduce their carbon footprint, this book demonstrates how. The result shows that flying less is not necessarily a hardship but can make both practical and personal sense. In particular, those authors who have drastically reduced their flying miles for work present a sound business case for many of their choices, and do not put them forward as heroic efforts to forgo the convenience of air travel.

The audience for *Beyond Flying* is the privileged few of the world's population who are rich enough to have the choice to fly. This small group has a choice whether to revel in their exclusive club and fly without worrying about the consequences, or to take action to force change on aviation. This book argues that each person should make a personal decision to fly less. Presented as a decision to fly or not to fly, this is a hard sell. But the chapters show that there are realistic alternatives.

Sustainable travel will be different, so the natural reaction of people is to resist; this is odd because a sustainable transport system will be better in almost every way. Before such a system can be built, this book provides pointers towards immediate action that every person can take. Such refusal to support the current model of aviation, if replicated widely, could help to drive change. If politicians found the courage to change policy, there could be a golden age of sustainable low-carbon aviation (McManners, 2012). There will be a small segment of people in senior positions who are time-poor and will continue to fly fast in aircraft, but they will pay a huge premium for the privilege. There will also be the rich, travelling in 'Premium Green' on board hybrid air vehicles (half aeroplane, half airship). Those of us on a tight budget will travel on 'Value Green', flying rather more slowly or using other means such as modern sailing ships or trains.

The transformation in aviation could take as little as five to ten years – if we had the will to change policy. The technology is understood and the designs are feasible, but in a world in which aviation fuel is constrained by international agreement to be tax-free, it is not commercially viable. The industry will not volunteer to change because much of the industry will collapse when society finally acts and existing fleets become obsolete. This should not be accepted as a reason for delay. Everyone should call on the politicians to find the courage to change international aviation agreements and force the industry to change.

Meanwhile, I detect little appetite for real action, despite evidence that the outcome is a better transport system. In addition to supporting my call for changing international aviation policy to provide the lever to transform the industry, each person can follow the examples in this book. Flying is for the rich world and the relatively rich in poorer countries, so there are no reasons for a special exemption. We need to push our politicians to act and, if you believe that climate change is an existential problem for our children and grandchildren, make the voluntary reductions in flying proposed here to reduce aviation emissions before it's too late.

Peter McManners
March 2013

References

McManners, P. J. (2012). *Fly and Be Damned: what now for aviation and climate change?* London: Zed Books.

Preface

It is said that a fish will be the last to discover water. And so it seems with airline passengers and the atmosphere. It is so easy to book flights, thinking about the destination ahead and what being there means to us, that we forget about the considerable effects of the pollution behind the aircraft and its impact on climate.

An uncomfortable feeling of hypocrisy arises when one attempts to reconcile environmental values with air miles and travel plans. In 2009 I was reassured to discover Flightless Birds, an online forum for conversations about making considered travel choices to avoid aviation pollution. Contributors cared enough about the future of the planet to make the overland journeys they described. In 2010 lawyer Tom Bennion and I developed the idea of this book, inspired by the realization that other people felt so strongly about the environment that they made conscious decisions to fly less.

As a *Guardian Weekly* subscriber, I was familiar with the writings of several authors who had explored sustainable travel. These writers enthusiastically accepted my invitation to contribute to the book by describing their personal and family history of flying, their circumstances of finding out about climate change, their adaptation to grounded modes of travel, and their experiences and learning gained along the way.

Beyond Flying describes how thinking changes among people who actively seek to minimize carbon emissions by flying less – or not at all. It looks at changes in values: from loving flying and all the experiences and relationships air travel enables, to appreciating other ways of connecting. It reports on changes in business and leisure activities and the reactions from friends and family when they learn that travellers are declining to take advantage of 'cheap' flights. Ultimately, by looking at these many facets of the decision to fly less, the authors are exploring the conundrum of living our globally connected lives with much less air travel.

This book is for people who travel, and for those who are thinking about the environment. The authors' stories illustrate new ways of thinking about flying. I hope these accounts will inspire readers to reconcile their own actions with their environmental values and promptly move their lives beyond flying.

Thanks to Whitireia Publishing for assistance with this project.

CW

Introduction

Chris Watson

Almost anyone can change their lifestyle to limit their carbon footprint to around one tonne CO_2-e (equivalent carbon dioxide) per year. The ways of minimizing energy consumption are simple and cost-effective. Efficiency strategies such as using well-designed buildings and public transport, cycling and eating local fruit and vegetables are simple and cost-effective, and have been proven over several decades. There are, however, no zero- or low-carbon options for aeroplane travel.

Despite the 1992 Earth Summit, aviation pollution has continued to increase because improvements in aircraft fuel efficiency have failed to keep up with the greater number of passengers flying further. Extreme weather events and the melting Arctic sea ice have been insufficient to prompt the industry to reduce its total pollution. It may never be possible for airlines to become substantially more efficient.

Biofuels are touted as a way of reducing emissions, but using agricultural land (which is already under strain from climate change) to produce fuel would take food from the mouths of hungry people. The only way to make the dramatic and immediate emission reductions necessary to address climate change is to adopt sufficiency strategies and develop new ways of thinking about long-distance connections and travel.

As some of the authors in this book describe, flying is an elite activity: only 5 per cent of people alive today have ever flown and, of those, very few are frequent flyers. It may be that just

1 per cent of humanity is responsible for 80 per cent of the world's flights. Thus there may be as few as 70 million frequent flyers who could quickly and dramatically reduce aviation's contribution to climate change by flying less.

Why do we fly? Of course it is enormously convenient. And it may offer enjoyment in itself as well as a quick and easy way to 'escape' our home lives. But there is more to it than that. Part of the answer might be that air travel seems to promise status to passengers. Philosopher Alain de Botton writes about the false dream of status arising from soaring above the clouds. Status-seeking may be part of the reason for weekend stag parties and shopping trips in foreign countries, or for so many face-to-face meetings with 'international experts' and conferences and holidays in exotic locations. To many, flying has simply become 'normal' – a habitual behaviour which allows us to conform with others in our social circle.

The authors in this book take us through the airline advertising myths and address aviation pollution as a personal issue; they don't blame the rich, the poor or any social or national group for climate change – they have set about minimizing their own air travel; their agenda is not 'climate change' but 'climate stabilization'. Throughout the book, the authors demonstrate various sustainable ways to maintain long-distance connections, and they reflect on the ways they value travel. Their transitions to less flying have been incremental shifts involving fewer flight bookings and increased use of sustainable transport and non-transport solutions. With the exception of emergencies, some authors have stopped flying completely.

Throughout the book, the authors show how it is possible to change the values and aspirations associated with air travel when its effect on climate change is understood. Indeed, the experience of these authors is that once they made the decision to fly less – in some sense to restrict their own freedom – they in fact felt freer, more open to new opportunities and more in tune with their own personal values. The authors also discuss their new ways of thinking about long-distance connections and strategies for moving beyond flying. In the first part of this book, authors describe their decisions to reduce or stop flying and offer their thoughts on alternative ways to travel. The second part is devoted to authors who have changed their business practices to reduce air travel. In the third part, authors describe long-distance overland journeys with the aim of inspiring in others the appreciation they found for slower, more grounded travel.

Chapter summaries
Part 1: Thinking beyond flying

Chris Brazier, a co-editor of *New Internationalist*, a magazine that reports on global justice issues and has offices in Europe, North America and Australasia, puts flying in the context of other environmental impacts. He reports on his company's initiative to take only six return flights per year. The chapter includes a ten-point plan to reduce flying.

Rob Hopkins is the co-founder of Transition Towns, a global movement of people adopting sustainable practices in preparation for declining oil supplies and to avoid contributing to climate change. He describes the impact of his 2006 decision never to fly again, made as part of his adoption of sustainable practices.

Saci Lloyd, best-selling author of the internationally acclaimed Carbon Diaries series, talks about inspiring young people to co-operate within egalitarian societies in order to stabilize the climate.

John Stewart, chair of the Heathrow Association for the Control of Aircraft Noise (HACAN), regularly travels around Europe by train. He discusses the productivity of working while travelling by train.

Kevin Anderson, deputy director of the Tyndall Centre for Climate Change Research, unpacks motivations for travel and questions whether so much of our travel is necessary. He examines air travel in terms of 'systems thinking', arguing that the benefits of not flying are of an order of magnitude greater than the mere savings in carbon of each avoided flight. He describes his week-long journey from Britain to China by the Trans-Siberian Express and the work opportunities this presented.

Part 2: Business beyond flying

Chris Watson developed his architectural practice with international contacts around the world. After reading extensively about climate change research he dramatically reduced business air travel and stopped almost all flying for holidays. He discusses the challenges this 'green travel' experiment has raised and the effective solutions he has found for doing international business without flying.

Kate Andrews travelled around the world by train, ship, yacht and bus before returning to London to establish a sustainable travel agency with her brother. She describes her mission of making rail travel booking easier and more price-competitive.

Tom Bennion is an environmental lawyer who has closely followed climate research and stopped all flying except for emergencies. He describes what that has meant for the way he practices law, and the effects on his business relationships and opportunities.

Susan Krumdieck, Associate Professor of Mechanical Engineering at the University of Canterbury in New Zealand, convened the Signs of Change teleconference, in which 250 delegates were hosted at seven venues. She offers a model for future e-conferences, describing how it was run and the significant savings in terms of time, costs and carbon emissions.

Ed Gillespie and his colleagues at Futerra, a London communications company, use trains for business travel in Europe in preference to flying. He describes how large organizations are doing business by videoconference and other means in order to reduce air travel.

Part 3: Savouring the journey

Chris Smith compares his cycle journey from Worcestershire to Beijing with the aircraft flight home. His 26,000-kilometre (16,000-mile) ride, powered by lungs and legs, energized him to deal with the unexpected challenges along the way. He says, 'the faster you travel the less you see'.

Adam Weymouth walked from England to Turkey, enjoying the richness of slow travel and observing how the landscape, vegetation and cultures subtly changed as he walked. He was humbled by the kindness of strangers, and engaged with everyone and everything he passed – something that is lost when one moves at a machine's speed.

Lowanna Doye and her partner Kevin cycled 12,000 kilometres (7,500 miles) from Oxford to Sydney, starting their bike2oz expedition in February 2000 and reaching Sydney in May 2001. They summed up the experience of travelling slowly across the surface of the Earth as 'the world going through you'.

Nic Seton travelled overland from Australia to a United Nations climate conference in Poland with members of the Australian Youth Climate Coalition. His reflections on the heavy cost to the planet of aviation are interspersed with vignettes of his remarkable journey and the encounters he had with local climate activists along the way.

Anirvan Chatterjee and **Barnali Ghosh** led conventional green lives in Berkeley, USA, until they discovered the damage caused by their flying. They describe their 'year of no flying', in which they travelled around the world by ship and train. In Thailand they met tourism researchers who exposed the dark side of the tourism industry, which brings locals plenty of misery but often very little reward.

How to fly less. After revealing some of the challenges and benefits of flying less, the book ends with a brief guide to ways in which you can reduce your own flying.

Part 1
Thinking beyond flying

1. To fly or not to fly?

Chris Brazier

This chapter originally appeared as an article in New Internationalist *magazine (Issue 409, 1 March 2008), www.newint.org*

Photo © Chris Brazier

Chris Brazier started his journalistic career at the rock music weekly *Melody Maker* in the late 1970s. Since 1984 he has been a co-editor at New Internationalist Publications, working on its monthly magazine about global justice issues as well as on its books. He writes regularly for UNICEF's State of the World's Children report and has authored books on topics as wide-ranging as *The No-Nonsense Guide to World History* and *Trigger Issues: Football*.

The plane is over the English Channel when the pilot's voice crackles over the loudspeakers. 'Just to warn you that there's been a bit of trouble at Heathrow with people protesting about the impact of air travel on climate change. Nothing to worry about, but when we land you may see a bigger police presence at the airport than you would normally expect.' The tone is jocular and clearly intended to draw us all together into a kind of community of 'sensible' travellers who might have to suffer the disruption of 'extremist' campaigners.

So what exactly am I doing here, in August 2007, given that I feel a much greater sense of kinship with the Climate Camp protesters below than with the pilot's cosy set of assumptions? It's a good question. My family and I are on our way back from a holiday in Italy. Last time we went, a few years ago, we drove there and back, via Luxembourg and Switzerland, taking our time and making many stop-offs on the way to break the journey. This time when we booked, almost a year in advance, we knew our holiday would be squeezed between work commitments and being back for our daughter's exam results. So, not without qualms, we took advantage of ludicrously cheap flights that would get us there in a couple of hours rather than a couple of days.

I tell you this to indicate my starting point when I began to research for this piece – for all that I bike to work, compost like crazy and am vegetarian, I am far from being in the environmental vanguard, and certainly don't feel able to lecture people about what they should or should not do.

Given this, I was not exactly burning to pick up the topic of ethical travel. I had no problem considering the effects of tourism on the Majority World (the so-called 'developing world'). But since most tourism depends on air travel, I knew I was likely to find myself in the unenviable position of having to offer readers some guidance on when flying is acceptable and when it isn't. And the more I sounded people out, the more my suspicions were confirmed. People are concerned and looking for guidance on an issue which has leapt to public attention in recent years – at least in Britain, where the debate about flying rages much hotter than it does in Australasia or North America.

Mind-boggling statistics

My early research left me shocked by the statistics on aviation emissions. Put simply, jet aircraft not only emit carbon from vast quantities of kerosene fuel, they also do it at high altitudes, where it has a much greater warming effect than it would in the lower atmosphere. In addition, jets emit other greenhouse gases, including nitrous oxide and water vapour ('contrails'). The Inter-governmental Panel on Climate Change (IPCC) estimates the net effect of all these emissions from jet aircraft at 2.7 times the carbon consumed in the fuel. An individual's share of carbon emitted on a return flight from London to New York (equivalent to 1,700 kg of CO_2) exceeds the carbon emitted by six months' worth of modest driving in an average car in the USA (equivalent to 1,650 kg of CO_2).

How such statistics are calculated is always a contentious issue. But the exact numbers are less interesting than the broad-brush comparisons: you can easily dump more carbon into the atmosphere from one return flight than from the gas and electricity you use in your house for an entire year. This was, to be frank, a mind-boggling discovery for me, which couldn't help but challenge my attitude to flying. Travel has played an enormous part in my life. I cannot easily conceive what kind of person I would be, had I not been able to board an aeroplane. But I do recognize that the profound implications of climate change (and the fight to prevent it) are going to force us all to take stock of our lives and challenge all our assumptions. Just how far, I wonder, are we prepared to go in challenging the flying culture?

My tentative proposal to the *New Internationalist* editorial team was that we should oppose the expansion of aviation – especially the development of new airports or runways – and encourage readers to reduce the amount they fly. But we should stop well short of calling for an end to all holiday flights.

A great deal of heat was generated in the discussion that ensued, but not a lot of light. It soon became plain that the issue of flying is a particularly thorny one, in which emotions are perhaps too readily engaged. And this was despite the fact that, perhaps surprisingly, there was no one in the room arguing that the magazine should rule out altogether flying for leisure or experience. One or two people argued that it would be so impossible to pin down reliable estimates of the emissions of various forms of transport that we would be treading on dodgy ground even to enter the flying debate.

There was also an argument that for the *New Internationalist* to concentrate its attention on individual behaviour – when and whether people should be travelling by plane – would be a mistake. There are much more important battles to be fought in the war on climate change, ran this strand of thought, than that of encouraging people to think about their 'carbon footprint'. I invited one of my editorial colleagues, Adam Ma'anit, to lay out this position.

Adam Ma'anit

I definitely agree with the need to deal with aviation's impact on climate change. My worry is about the focus on individual consumption, on individuals taking flights. I think the emphasis needs to go back towards political, economic and environmental policies. Too much of the flying debate is about individual one-upmanship and not about real substantive change. It's natural for the environmental movement to go down that path because it's easier to appeal to their base – environmentally minded folk who will accept the wisdom of flying less and peer-pressure each other – but the movement shouldn't shy away from the difficult questions.

Lifestyle politics may be a hit with the hair-shirt crowd, but it's small fry compared with the huge socio-political changes needed to avert the worst excesses of climate change. Just as telling people to eat better won't solve the obesity crisis, so too will the 'you fly, we die' message fall on deaf ears. And let's not forget the importance of building up the alternatives. Telling people to fly less and travel by train instead when the rail system in many countries is so mind-bogglingly expensive, overcrowded and unreliable is hardly a convincing argument. Rather than solely appealing to people's better consciences, let's focus our energies on the big wins that can be made with modest political will.

Aviation's growth is very worrying and that does need to be curtailed. The big target is short-haul flights to destinations that could easily and comfortably be serviced by rail, bus or ferry. But those services need to run well, they need to be just as heavily scrutinized for their environmental impacts and they should be reasonably affordable and safe. At the moment, they're often not, so it's no wonder people take to the skies. But not flying has become an iconic badge of environmental commitment, and I think that's misguided.

If there was the political will to do something about climate change, so much could be done in so little time and aviation would play a relatively small role in reducing the global footprint. For example, if government said tomorrow, 'we're going to ban all electronic devices with standby mode' it would reduce electricity consumption by a huge amount at a stroke. How many people factor the standby mode into their purchasing decisions? Not many. But if you deal with it at a macro level you actually take it out of the equation.

It's the same with government-sponsored housing insula-
tion, combined heat and power units for residential
blocks, support for micro-renewables. Curtailing military
activities would deliver massive carbon savings and free
up resources that could be used to steer us away from
climate disaster. There are lots of things that simply can't
be done at an individual level and have to be done by
society as a whole – reining in corporate power and
wasteful energy transmission, decentralising energy grids
and promoting renewables, stopping subsidies of fossil
fuels, ending aviation's tax-free fuel ride. And that's just
for starters... There is so much we can do now. So let's
stop the incessant navel-gazing and agonising over our
personal carbon 'footprints' and build the momentum for
real change.

There is no doubt that the primary need is for governments,
rather than individuals, to take action. Climate change is the
greatest issue of our time, yet politicians the world over continue
to funk it, fearing that if they derail the globalised consumer
bandwagon it will cost them their jobs. Given how huge the task
is in front of us, the primary requirement has to be to campaign,
to do all we can to change the political landscape so that it
reflects the real (planet-) burning issues rather than the pre-
eminent concern with the dollar in our pocket.

But I still feel it is important to include in this article some rec-
ognition of the dilemma faced by individual readers concerned
about the ethics of flying in an overheating world. Those of us
who try to reduce or constrain our carbon footprint are not
likely to be distracted from campaigning for the big-picture
political changes. One can reinforce the other. Don't we all feel
much more comfortable campaigning for a cause if we are doing
our bit? That way at least we can't be charged with hypocrisy.

And our own individual actions may have a ripple effect, whether by inspiring others or by contributing to a statistical trend. Changing our lifestyle could reinforce pressure on politicians to pull us out of this tailspin. After all, we know more clearly than ever that every kilogram of carbon we propel into the atmosphere is doing some very dirty work.

Consulting the oracles

One of the main proponents of the 'carbon footprint' way of looking at this problem is Mark Lynas, author of *High Tide: News from a Warming World*, *Six Degrees: Our Future on a Hotter Planet* and *Carbon Calculator: Easy Ways to Reduce your Carbon Footprint*. When I met Mark, he was just back from a mammoth journey by boat to Norway. 'It took ten days – it was a disaster,' he said ruefully. 'If I'd done it in a plane trip in a day it would have been a hell of a lot easier than dragging the whole family out there for ten days. You can go a bit too far in terms of being puritan on this. Mind you, it always pays off because people always ask how you got there. And it's nice to be able to say: "Well, train and boat!" It even makes headlines in the papers because people don't expect it.'

While he has ruled out holiday flights for himself, he readily acknowledges the moral complexity of the issue – as well as stressing that he too sees individual effort as secondary to the vital job of building a movement that will shift governments. And he hankers after a techno fix, even though, he added, 'George will kill me for saying so'.

The George in question is Monbiot, the *Guardian* columnist and author of Heat: How we can stop the planet burning (Monbiot, 2007). The chapter on aviation ('Love Miles') lays out very starkly the damage done by air travel – and the impossibility of meeting any meaningful emissions targets if we continue our love affair with it.

> A 90 per cent cut in carbon emissions means the end of distant foreign holidays, unless you are prepared to take a long time getting there … It means that journeys around the world must be reserved for visiting the people you love, and that they will require both slow travel and the saving up of carbon rations … If you fly, you destroy other people's lives.

Gulp. You can't get much more categorical than that.

George Monbiot

It's possible to have a technological effect on almost every other area of climate change apart from aviation. You could run almost the entire energy system on renewable power if you did it in the right way. Aviation is the one area for which there is no available technological solution in the foreseeable future. We're not likely to see battery-powered jetliners.

It's not just a question of blocking future airport expansion; we have to reduce what's already there. We have to cut aviation emissions by 95 per cent if we're going to keep overall emissions to the level we need to. That means people can fly only 5 per cent of the amount they are now – and that's a maximum.

People shouldn't be flying for leisure or tourism purposes at all. They also shouldn't be flying for business. If you've got a pressing family obligation, a relative who's sick or dying, then fair enough. And if you're doing something important with human rights or raising awareness of the environmental threat and there's no other way of getting there, you might be able to justify it. But even then you have to think very carefully because it's going to be rare that the importance of the work will outweigh the damage done by the flight.

What about damage done to communities in the Majority World that are currently dependent on tourism?

I do accept that some communities are going to be hit hard by this. But you have to set that against the enormous and much greater damage that will be done to other communities all over the world by climate change. We have to make it a priority to help those communities and countries to develop better ways of surviving and thriving that do not depend upon transporting 150 pounds of human halfway across the planet and back.

What would the world be like without the intercultural exchanges that derive from air travel?

Cross-cultural international connections don't depend entirely on flying. You can travel by boat or by train almost anywhere – it just takes a lot more time. So travelling without flying is still possible.

And in terms of bringing about change, it isn't really necessary to travel to become an internationalist. At the time of the Make Poverty History campaign [a campaign by a coalition of charities, religious groups, trades unions, campaigning groups and celebrities at the time of the G8 Summit in Edinburgh in 2005], most of the people in the West who became deeply concerned about Africa had never visited there but had been moved by what they had seen on television. You don't become an internationalist by travelling – just as travelling in itself doesn't make you an internationalist.

You started as a travel writer, though. You've benefited in all kinds of ways from international travel that have helped make you the person you are. How can you deny those benefits to young people now?

I do feel bad that I have to say to young people now that they cannot have the opportunities I had for guilt-free experience of other lands and cultures. But there's no alternative. That experience of travel is simply not available to people now. It's another example of how the sins of one generation have been handed to the next generation, who have to pay the price.

You might wonder why I didn't ask the most obvious follow-up question: how many times have you yourself flown somewhere in the last year? Actually I didn't need to ask – Monbiot was so primed for that question that he misheard one of my others and answered that he has taken two flights in the previous 18 months, both of them to climate-change events where he judged that he could make more of a difference by attending in person than by not flying.

I was more concerned to probe how he, who began as a travel writer and has benefited in all kinds of ways from experiencing other countries and cultures, feels able to say that young people now should not avail themselves of the same opportunities. He successfully conveys that however bad he feels about it, the problem is so huge and so all-trumping that there is simply no alternative.

I cannot bring myself to say the same. As I write, my daughter is experiencing her first day of teaching in a village in Malawi, having just spent a week of 'orientation' in the capital, Lilongwe. I am proud that she has chosen to spend her gap year working in Africa. What she learns about the world and its injustices and inequalities will reverberate through her entire life and will give her a connection with Malawi, and with Africa as a whole, that no amount of book reading or film watching could have achieved. Should I really have said to her, at a time when the rest of the world seems to be leaping on a plane at the drop of a hat to sun themselves on a beach or to go shopping, that she should forego the whole experience because we have just begun to understand the climate-changing contribution of aviation? I don't think so.

What would happen in a no-fly world?

What would happen at *New Internationalist* if we introduced a no-flying policy? The issue has already caused some soul-searching within the cooperative. People travelling to the annual Frankfurt Book Fair, for example, have had to weigh the environmental impact against the cost (since the advent of budget airlines, ridiculously enough it is actually cheaper to fly from Britain to Germany than to go by train) and the significant extra time involved. Even if a company has a policy that supports (and is prepared to pay for) an employee wishing to go overland, there are often family or work reasons why that person is loath to be away longer than need be.

Given that we have editors in Canada, Australia and Holland, and that we focus on the concerns of the Majority World, eschewing flying altogether does not seem to be an option for us as an organization. Certainly the need for editors to be in touch with the realities of everyday life in Africa, Asia and Latin America – on which the magazine's reputation stands – depends on their being able to hear ordinary people's testimonies first-hand rather than just relying on printed reports or local journalists.

And *New Internationalist* is, after all, only the tip of the 'One World community' iceberg, which has been founded on international travel in both directions – on people visiting and migrating to our own countries from far-flung locations, and on our learning from and adjusting to other peoples and cultures. What would happen to a world in which the only people who travelled by plane were those most committed to its rapacious exploitation? Would airways become the de facto province of the most unscrupulous corporations? Besides, where is the sense in rejecting one aspect of international aviation (tourism) while accepting other aspects (air-freighted goods and foodstuffs, air mail, and so on)?

No more new runways

In the context of an ever-warming world, if we continue to fly for our pleasure and education, we need to ensure that tourism is not itself damaging, and that it genuinely benefits the host communities at the other end. It also means we have to increase pressure on policymakers to contain and reduce air travel. Governments all too readily point the finger at individuals rather than demonstrating leadership on the matter. I encountered an example of this recently when, at a Christmas party, I got talking to a civil servant working on transport problems. I was explaining why I thought the British government's intention to build a third runway at Heathrow to meet anticipated demand was the purest folly. 'It's not up to the government to take a lead on this issue,' he said. 'It's up to individuals to stop taking advantage of cheap flights.'

As an evasion of responsibility, this takes some beating. Yet it mirrors the approach of most Western governments, which simply puts a blind eye to the telescope and continues to chase economic growth whatever the environmental cost. Pointing to booming demand, they plan for new runways and new airports that will soon fill to capacity just like the extra lane for cars on an expressway. As a result, air travel is growing at a rate of some 5 per cent a year, meaning that air passenger kilometres are set to triple by 2030 (Rice-Oxley, 2007).

Air travel urgently needs to be contained – and physical limits (not enough runways to meet demand) are actually a very practical, sensible method of containment. It also doesn't take an expert to see that the current convenient practice of excluding international air travel from all national emissions targets is absurdly ostrich-like. Besides, the boom in air travel cannot be accounted for by 'ordinary hard-working people taking their one holiday a year', which is the routine claim of the media and the travel industry. British government statistics show that 62 per cent of adults did not make even one return flight in 2006. Among the richest 20 per cent of the population, 61 per cent took one or more return flights. Only 4 per cent of people took four or more flights ([UK] Department for Transport, 2006).

So even in the rich world, we are talking about a tiny minority of people who may be flying an insane amount. Below are a suggested 'Ten steps to reduce flying' – and some of these will affect only that tiny minority. But others will apply to you and me as well, because even if the primary focus has to be on forcing governments into action, we still need to do our individual bit.

In a way, putting this piece together has been a gesture in this direction since, three trips to London by train and bus aside, I have made a point of avoiding travelling (always, depressingly, the most ethical course of action of all). On the home front, my family has already decided to holiday this year in Cornwall, on the English coast, rather than further afield. But, on the other hand, the following year we have long planned to revisit friends and familiar places in Canada – we lived in Toronto for a year in the mid-1990s. And now my brother's family is on the verge of emigrating to Australia – so without one or other of us flying we would never see each other again.

New Internationalist policy on flying

The New Internationalist cooperative has since agreed to use alternatives to air travel whenever possible and has set a target of no more than six return trips per year, with the aim of reducing this number. Three flights are set aside for editorial research, with the remaining flights to be used for other business activities. Staff are supported in using alternatives to air travel by being encouraged to allow extra time for their journey, by being provided with technology that enables them to work while travelling and being given time off in lieu for out-of-hours work. In all but the most exceptional circumstances, meetings with offices in different countries are conducted on a 'virtual' basis. In practice, since this policy was adopted, in no year has the flight quota been exceeded and in most years it has been significantly undershot.

It's a tangled web, as this article – if it has done nothing else – has made plain. Good luck to all of you as you try to sort out what you think about it.

Ten steps to reducing flying

Rule out commuting by air

A no-brainer for most of us but increasing numbers of people are actually doing this. Once almost entirely a North American phenomenon, cheap air travel has now produced the equivalent in Australasia and Europe. Air commuting tends to be a weekly rather than a daily occurrence, but none of the reasons for entertaining this – high property prices where you work, a long-distance lover – could possibly render it justifiable in ethical terms. Either be content where you are or emigrate – but don't imperil us all by living in one country and working in another. And in the unlikely event we have a reader with a private jet, please contact the New Internationalist for better ideas as to how to spend your money.

Think again about that holiday home

Again, most people can jump to the next step. But for those to whom this applies… OK, so this might have seemed a good idea at the time – 'we'll have a foothold in an area we love', 'it's a good investment', 'it'll be something to pass on to the kids', and so on. But if it depends on cheap air travel to reach the place, this is an edifice built on sand. Any kind of second home (let alone third or fourth) is bound to increase your carbon contribution massively, even if it is reachable by car or train.

Find alternatives to flying for work

Flying is built into some people's jobs. And in some cases it's necessary – if someone's writing a report about poverty in the Philippines, say, the *New Internationalist* would be the first to protest if they tried to do so without leaving Washington, DC. Sometimes there is no substitute for being in the same room. But such occasions are pretty rare in the age of digital communication. Many flights for work are actually little more than perks. Transnationals have long been able to afford videoconferencing, but the advent of Skype and Second Life means that even humble outfits like the New Internationalist can now have regular international meetings without even incurring the cost of a phone call.

Cut out weekend jaunts and 'city breaks'

Low-cost travel, particularly in Europe, has brought with it a
new phenomenon – people who fly off to Madrid or Prague or
the Baltic states for the weekend. Given that short-haul flights
are more damaging (because take-off and landing consume
much more fuel than cruising at high altitude), this is environmentally disastrous. Some people have added a weekend break
away in spring and maybe a skiing holiday in winter to the two
weeks in the summer sun that used to be the limit of their
expectations. In addition, stag/bachelor/buck parties that once
meant a night out on the town can now involve a weekend in a
foreign capital.

Use land travel where possible

Trains, buses and cars make their own carbon contribution. But as
a broad rule of thumb, any trip overland is far less damaging than
one by air – with the possible exceptions of a sleeper compartment on a train or an SUV carrying only the driver. Car journeys
consume broadly the same carbon as would a flight over the same
distance, so if they are shared with others they come out better.
And in a car, bus or train at least we notice the ground covered.
Hop on a plane and we are magically removed from real time, real
travel – and from any sense of connection with our carbon impact.

Campaign against airport expansion

We know from experience that if a road is widened to reduce
congestion, more cars will simply fill up the space. The same
applies to airports. Lack of runway space is a physical limit on air
travel that we desperately need to retain. OK so you may have to
travel a few hours to a plane because your local airport has not
been allowed to expand – but look at the bigger picture and this
is a very small price to pay.

Enjoy travelling slowly

The idea of slow travel is beginning to gain credence, mirroring the 'slow food' movement (originating in Italy) that values food from local artisans rather than the mass-produced, industrially processed mainstream variety. 'Slow travel' might involve redis-covering the delights of the long train journey – communicating with the diverse people who spend time in your carriage and watching the landscapes and communities change instead of leaping over them in one bound. The transcontinental train journey across Canada, for example, is wondrous – yet relatively few Canadians actually make it.

Holiday closer to home

Exotic holidays in far-off places can, of course, be memorable experiences. But holidays in your own country can be just as relaxing. Why not take a break from flying and only holiday in an exotic locale every other year, or one year in three? That way, not only will you contribute less carbon but the trip itself will be more special. The Australasian tradition of one long 'grand tour' undertaken before responsibilities kick in is a sensible way of dealing with geographic isolation – provided it does not involve too many unnecessary flights. If you've taken a year out of your life to travel, you have the time to travel overland.

Don't offset, join the campaign

Instead of offsetting, just try to cut out a future flight. Offsetting projects are often dubious – at their worst they involve requiring people in the Majority World not to use technology in compen-sation for our using it to the max. And offsets are all too often a convenient let-out for a travel industry unwilling to deal with the real implications of climate change. If you must go ahead, make sure you know what the offset company is doing with the money – and don't assume it lets you off the hook of campaigning against climate change and reducing your own footprint.

Take the pledge

The Flight Pledge Union offers you the chance to pledge not to travel by air for a year except in an emergency. This is the 'gold' pledge. The 'silver' version is much more modest, involving a promise not to take more than two short-haul return flights or one long-haul return flight in the year to come. Pledges like this can raise awareness and increase commitment. But they are not the be-all and end-all – use them to help you feel more comfortable about campaigning for the big-picture changes that governments and industries urgently need to make.

References

Department for Transport (2006). *Transport Statistics Bulletin National Travel Survey: 2006*. London: Department for Transport.

Monbiot, G. (2007). *Heat: How we can stop the planet burning*. London: Penguin.

Rice-Oxley, M. (2007). 'Air travel latest target in climate change fight'. *Christian Science Monitor*. Retrieved from www.csmonitor.com/2007/0817/p01s01-woeu.html

2. Deciding never to fly again

Rob Hopkins

Rob Hopkins is co-founder of the Transition Town movement and author of *The Transition Handbook* and *The Transition Companion*. He lectures and writes widely on peak oil and transition, holds an MSc in Social Research, and recently completed a PhD on localisation and resilience. He is now a Visiting Fellow at the University of Plymouth. He lives in Devon, grows food for his family and blogs at transitionnetwork.org/blogs/rob-hopkins

Photo © Stephen Prior, Green Books

In August 2006, my family and I made the decision to stop flying. I don't know why it took so long really, but finally we agreed that we wouldn't fly any more. I had one flight booked already that I was committed to, but beyond that we planned to travel using our van or by train – or to stay at home. The reasons were legion, and I'm sure readers know most of them already. What is more telling was the process by which we finally decided to stop flying, despite having talked about it for years.

I often hear it said that 'people won't change until it is too late' or 'people don't change until they have to', both statements I have always instinctively disagreed with but haven't quite known why. One of the insights I gleaned from William R. Miller and Stephen Rollnick's book *Motivational Interviewing* – a very insightful approach to working with addiction – is that this is nonsense. If it were true then there would be no recovered addicts anywhere; they would all have died. Miller and Rollnick argue in their book that people change when they can no longer support the discrepancy between their core values and what they are doing (Miller and Rollnick, 2002).

I have written previously about chef Jamie Oliver's School Dinners TV series, which is a great example of developing awareness of that kind of discrepancy (Hopkins, 2006). When he says, 'This is the first generation that will die before its parents', he shows that a core value of people (that their kids should be healthy and live longer than them) is wildly out of step with reality. Oliver encouraged his viewers to reach a point where they could no longer support a particular behaviour. So it was with us and flying.

It's not that we were serial flyers; we flew perhaps once a year. The thing that finally developed the required degree of discrepancy for us was an article in the *Telegraph* in July 2006. Entitled 'Why we must give up flying', it was written by geographer and journalist Nicholas Crane. In 1988 Crane had been so shocked by a lecture on climate change given at the Royal Geographical Society that he began to question his role in encouraging thousands of people through his articles to fly to faraway destinations. He reported being 'wracked with guilt' about the behaviour he was encouraging. In 1995 he decided that he had to give up flying. Two years later he took his last flight as a travel writer. He went on to describe how he had adapted to working as a non-flying journalist, including producing a TV series on British landscapes. Crane wrote the article after hearing that the bishop of London had declared casual long-distance travel to be sinful. As Crane put it,

But how big a personal price is this, really? A long time

ago, I rode a bicycle through Bangladesh. On dirt roads between paddy fields, my cousin and I pedalled alongside throngs of laughing children. We ate curries in shacks while entire villages turned out to admire our bikes. Much of Bangladesh will be flooded before the end of the century. Millions of Bangladeshis will become homeless. How can I look a Bangladeshi in the eye and claim a right to fly? (Crane, 2006)

It seemed it was not just me moving away from air travel and stressful hours in airports. I remember seeing a headline in the *Independent* that read 'The great British holiday boom', leading an article about the fact that due to rising air prices, airport delays, and somewhat dubious 'security alerts' at Heathrow, people in the UK were deciding to holiday in the UK. Finding accommodation in Cornwall was, apparently, tough going (Brown, Jack and Shah, 2006). Fantastic, I say.

One of the things that struck me during my 'to fly or not to fly' deliberations was that despite the fact that the UK is one of the world's most popular tourist resorts, I hardly knew it at all. I had never been to Dorset or the Norfolk Broads; my geography of north of Birmingham was sketchy, and I had never been to the north-east at all. The British grumble about how bad the weather is, how cold and rainy it is all winter, and then as soon as it gets to be summer they jet off overseas. Looks like all this is starting to change, and not a day too soon.

In the six years since I made the decision not to fly, I have not set foot on an aeroplane. I have travelled from London to the north of Scotland on a sleeper train with my 14-year-old son. When we awoke we were travelling through the Highlands, which were thick with snow. We put our hands out of the window to catch and taste snowflakes. I have travelled to a conference in Pisa on the sleeper train – an absolute joy – watching the landscapes and cultures change, meeting great people and experiencing the camaraderie of a shared couchette, fellow travellers pooling their food for an impromptu potluck supper. I have been to Austria, up in the mountains, drinking Austrian beer on a train heading into an Alpine sunset and eating early-morning pizza on a small station famed for being home to one of the first local currency experiments in the 1930s.

I work for Transition Network, supporting initiatives in 34 countries that encourage communities to see the localisation of their economies as a huge opportunity, where local food, community-owned energy and social enterprises are central to their economic development. I do a lot of public speaking on the subject, usually setting out what Transition is and how to do it. I have spoken about Transition at conferences and events in Australia, the USA, Canada, Spain, the Czech Republic, Croatia and New Zealand, to name but a few, and all without leaving my small office in Devon, once described by the *Sunday Telegraph* as 'a rickety set of rooms'. Either we pre-record talks and send the DVD, or I speak using Skype or other conferencing packages, which become better all the time. It has been reported that several of these pre-recorded talks that I have opened with an explanation of why I'm not there in person and how much carbon has been saved have been given standing ovations.

My favourite story is when we had a phone call from California, from the organizers of the Curry Stone Design Prize. 'You are a finalist in the Curry Stone Design Prize!' they said. 'You need to come to California for the prize-giving ceremony.' I explained that I didn't fly and couldn't attend in person. 'But you have to come, you're a finalist,' they said. I restated that while I was thrilled to hear that we were a finalist, I felt that the very reasons why they considered our work worthy of being a finalist were the same reasons why I wouldn't be flying to California, and that perhaps given that we were a finalist, they might work out a way to weave that in and celebrate it. 'We'll get back to you,' they said. Two weeks later they rang to tell me that all four finalists would be presenting by Skype.

You may think that such an approach must surely have limited the spread of the Transition idea. Shortly before the Copenhagen conference in December 2009, I asked the Transition Network for their thoughts on my non-flying stance and whether the organization as a whole should make that commitment. One correspondent laid out a detailed argument for not doing so. He made the point that, while a ban on flying would lower the carbon footprint of our organization, it would prevent valuable work and remove an important choice for individuals working for our organization. He concluded:

> Where this leaves me is that to be a truly alive organisation we need to be living Transition, and that means we – all of us – have to face making the sorts of (often) least-bad choices in living everyday life. I would hope we all have the awareness and understanding that this is what 'living Transition' means; at least while we still have choice. When we no longer have a choice, then Transition turns into something else. I personally think that there are times you should go somewhere and speak even if it means flying, as you can be very inspirational (as it is having a deeply held belief – as you do – that you don't fly).

In response I outlined my view with the following points. First, Transition is, at its core, about preparing, positively and imaginatively, as well as with a considerable sense of urgency, for a world beyond fossil-fuel dependency. The idea of striving to live as though we were already there feels like an important one to me. It seems critical that we get ahead of the curve in terms of thinking, and modelling how an organization that has an international reach, but in which noone flies, might work.

Second, if Transition Network decided collectively that no one representing them should ever fly, we should wear that with pride. If a tree falls in a forest and nobody sees it, it may just as well not have bothered. In the same way, if I spend hours on trains to Austria and back and don't tell people about it, it has a fraction of the impact. I felt that if the Network decided collectively to have a no-flying policy, it should be writ bold and clear that so concerned were we about climate change, and so determined to start modelling post-oil practices today, that we had collectively decided not to fly, and we should explain how it had improved our quality of life as an organization.

I was increasingly disillusioned by the army of climate experts and sustainability advisers who were continually flying from conference to conference. I felt that Transition Network should be modelling a different approach, if for no other reason than because nobody else was. Saying 'we think in principle that flying isn't great, but everyone should be able to decide on a case -by-case basis' was reminiscent of lots of corporate green wish lists, voluntary green commitments and 'carbon friendly' type greenwash. It could be used to cover a multitude of sins, and it hardly represented best practice. In the end, the decision was taken to not fly unless the case could be made that flying (for example to give Transition training) would prevent a far greater number of people flying in the opposite direction.

As I write in 2012, the Transition movement has spread to 34 countries, with many thousands of initiatives. It has won awards and was recently referred to by the same Nicholas Crane on BBC2 as 'the biggest urban brainwave of the century'. We have 'walked the talk' in a way that many people admire. We have tried to move away from the model of a 'guru flying around the world', and instead enabled a self-organizing movement that pops up in the most unexpected places.

At least twice a week I get requests to travel to different parts of the world to teach, give talks or meet Transition groups. Any that would necessitate plane travel are politely told that I don't fly, but that we would be delighted to set up some sort of video link. Of course it's not quite the same quality of experience as my being there in person, but it does, for me, have the strong advantage of being low-carbon, replicable and far less time-consuming than flying, and it sends a powerful message as well as setting an example.

I don't try in any sense to fool myself that my giving up flying is going to reverse climate change. I don't think as I cycle to work or as I stand at Cologne train station that some miraculous process is taking place, ice sheets magically refreezing and glaciers expanding. For me, not flying is not about thinking that by giving it up I am having a big impact on the world. Rather it is underpinned by Vandana Shiva's thought that 'these systems exist because we give them our support, and if we withdraw that support they can no longer function' (Shiva, 2005). My not flying makes little difference, but Ryanair no longer existing would make some difference. It's the bit I can do. Withdrawal of support is a powerful tool – the impact of which we often underestimate.

I remember one meeting of European Ashoka Fellows in Austria (a fellowship of social entrepreneurs of which I am a member). I travelled there and back by train, the only person who did. Everyone attending had been told in advance about this mad bloke who was travelling there by train from England, and it was the subject of much discussion, with lots of people really admiring the stance.

So have I lost anything through not flying? Do I pine for the far-flung corners of the world that I will never see, for Mount Kailash in Tibet – the one place I have always wanted to visit? Giving up flying has never felt like giving up anything. It is true that I don't have relatives around the world, and so George Monbiot's 'love miles' aren't an issue for me. If one of my sons moved to live in New Zealand with a family, my views on flying might find themselves sorely tested.

But, if anything, giving up flying has led to my feeling more rooted, more mindful of distances and aware of the fact that 'far away' really is indeed quite far away. I remain shocked at people I know, who imagine themselves as environmentally aware, going to India to do a course for two weeks, or visiting the USA for a week's break. I am shocked too by the friend who told me, unaware of the irony, that she was flying to New Mexico for 'an Earth Wisdom retreat'. I'd like to think that, in a quiet way, my giving up flying has been my own kind of 'Earth Wisdom retreat': a retreat from an unnecessarily high-carbon lifestyle, which has allowed me to develop a deeper mindfulness of the world beneath my feet and the true nature of distance. It has also led me to discover the world around me in a far more meaningful way. And I don't need to go to New Mexico for that.

Addendum

As described above, in 2006 I gave up flying, a determined decision to 'walk my talk' and to model the building of an international network of communities without the need for constant air travel. The subsequent spread of Transition Network has been supported via webinars, filmed talks and presentations, videoconferencing, blogs and books. I am told that this approach has inspired many other people to stop flying, has saved thousands of tonnes of carbon, and has shown that there are viable alternatives to air travel.

In 2013 I went to a screening of the film *Chasing Ice*, which topped up my sense of the deeply urgent nature of the climate crisis and gave me a visceral feeling that everything we're doing, is still not enough. Shortly afterwards, I received an invitation from the USA and decided, after much soul-searching, to make one trip to try and contribute to shifting the debates there. What swung it was that I had a deeply moving conversation with a leading US climate activist, funder and networker, who stated that many leading organizations now talk of giving climate mitigation just 18-24 months before putting all funding and resources into climate adaptation and defence. For me, the conversation was a tipping point. On my blog, reflecting on the decision to get back on a plane one last time, I wrote,

> What haunts me every day, and no doubt will for the rest of my days, is what I will reply to my grandchildren when they ask me what I did during the time when climate change could have been brought under some sort of control, when the necessary changes could have been put in place to create a low-carbon, resilient and thriving culture that nurtured healthy human cultures. Was I as effective as I could have been? Did I do everything I could have? Having reflected on this for some time, it feels churlish to decline an opportunity that could potentially have far greater positive impact than the negative impact of the flight.

Although aware that the USA is already home to a dazzling array of initiatives, inspiring speakers and thinkers and deeply committed changemakers, my hope is that bringing the experience of the Transition movement, now active in 34 countries, and the story it has to tell about the scale of the change local communities can enable, could have some influence on debates and action at both local and national level. Whether it will or not, I shall never know. I see this very much as a one-off. I guess this leaves my contribution here ending rather conflicted, but given the scale of this crisis, we all have to do what we can, and this piece has documented my own personal struggle with this. I hope it helps you with yours!

References

Brown, J., Jack, L. and Shah, S. 'The great British holiday boom'. *Independent*, 19 August, 2006. Retrieved from www.independent.co.uk/news/uk/this-britain/the-great-british-holiday-boom-412476.html

Crane, N. 'Why we should cut down on flying'. *Telegraph*, 29 July, 2006. Retrieved from www.telegraph.co.uk/travel/735900/Why-we-should-cut-down-on-flying.html

Hopkins, R. (2006). 'What can we learn from Jamie's school dinners? – 10 insights for energy descent'. Retrieved from http://transitionculture.org/2006/07/06/what-can-we-learn-from-jamies-school-dinners-10-insights-for-energy-descent/

Miller, W. and Rollnick, S. (2002). *Motivational Interviewing: Preparing people for change* (2nd edn). New York: Guilford Press

Shiva, V. (2005). *Earth Democracy: Justuce, sustainability and peace*. London: Zed Books

3. Young people and climate change

Saci Lloyd Interview by Chris Watson via Skype

Photo © Emli Bendixen

Saci Lloyd is a children's writer and teacher. She was born in Manchester and brought up in Anglesey, Wales. After leaving university for a life of glamour, she has worked at various times as a very bad cartoonist, toured the USA in a straight-edge band, run an interactive media team at an advertising agency, co-founded a film company, and finally wound up as head of media at a sixth form college in east London. Lloyd's first novels, the *Carbon Diaries* series, met with critical acclaim. Her book *Momentum* was released in 2011, and *Quantum Drop* was released in 2013.

Where did you grow up?

I grew up in Anglesey, an island off north-west Wales, where as a kid I spent a lot of time lost in nature or down by the shore. It is a real contrast to where I live now on the outskirts of London, although I have some connection with nature as we live on the edge of Epping Forest. But I miss the countryside.

Tell us about your early experiences of flying.

My family was lower middleclass; when I was a child, holidays abroad were for a few lucky kids from wealthy families. None of the kids in my class had been outside Wales by the age of 12, which is incredible now, I suppose. Anyway, we lived on a beautiful island so we did not need to go anywhere else.

I remember we flew to Spain when I was very little. It was the beginning of 'bucket shop' holidays – you know, the cheap package holidays to the south of Spain, Majorca, and so on.

If you look at attitudes towards the UK as a place to have a holiday, it is interesting to see how much that has changed. Package holidays have made us appreciate Britain less because air travel has opened up new worlds. When we flew less, we were so hopeful and lively about our weather. I remember as soon as the sun came out, it was 'go go go' – enjoy it because it might only last a few hours. We have become so emotionally dependent on the idea of hot weather somewhere else.

How did you first become concerned about the environmental impacts of flying?

I was lying on a beach in Thailand reading George Monbiot's book *Heat* while researching my second book. I read the chapter on flying with a sinking heart. Before that I had flown quite a lot. I had an Australian partner and so had made four to five round trips to Australia and flown around Europe. I just didn't know [about the impact of aviation on the environment]. I don't feel guilty now, but once you are presented with the facts and realize [the impact of aviation], you have to take some kind of action.

There are many ways we burn fossil fuels, such as cars and electricity from coal. Why is less flying so important to you?

I feel sorry for the aviation industry in a way. Their engineers have made huge advances in efficiency. Aircraft are so much cleaner than they were, but the basic physics of flying means that there is a limit to how much more efficient they can be. Burning fuel in the sky is so much worse in terms of pollution at ground level; it has two to three times the [forcing] effect.

I was in Sinai when the Icelandic volcano erupted in 2010: I think 26,000 flights per day were disrupted and Europe had a breathing space of three to four days. Yet all the media coverage focused on stranded holidaymakers, or how bad this was for business. There was no debate about the craziness of the system.

Why did you first write about climate change for young people?

I just write books: they are not particularly for young people. I think these stories about climate change are the great stories of the age. There are seven billion people on the planet. We are so dominant that we are now affecting sea and sky.

I think it is a very exciting time. I am interested in the real story of humanity. It has become very clouded in the last couple of hundred years.

There is an assumption that we own the earth and we can trash it. But I feel the real story of us is one of egalitarianism and cooperation. And all of our great technological and social advances emerge from this spirit. We're all standing on the shoulders of people before us.

But now, in the early twenty-first century, capitalism has started to eat itself. We have forgotten our history and we need urgently to revive a sense of stewardship.

We are a unique animal. Through design and words, we play with ideas before we turn them into a reality. This is what I'm doing with my writing: creating a space for readers to explore the ideas around climate change. I am very interested in scenarios where you squeeze young characters and see the response.

What are young people thinking about climate change?

There is a diverse mix of reactions. It is still seen as a middle-class issue. But I think the movement is broadening and now there is a much wider range of young people becoming very bothered.

In my work I try to create a progressive vision of what it means to bring about change. I talk about young people being pioneers – riding a new wave of dynamic thinking and leaving the old, carbon-heavy ways behind.

I think that gradually we are moving to a different way of owner-ship, and in the future we will either process goods cradle-to-cradle – or have a few objects we make personal and beautiful and long-lasting. We don't have to have the endless throwaway culture.

These are the messages, the ideas that get young people excited. They want to move forward, but they need a progressive modern vision, not some dour tale about giving up all their possessions and paying for their parents' mistakes.

What reactions have you had to your books?

The reaction around the world has been very, very positive. The *Carbon Diaries 2015* has been translated into 15 languages, and *Momentum* has been selling very well. It has been put in the UK school curriculum.

The books look at the effects of climate change in our everyday lives – in our streets. I think people are able to relate to that.

When did you first realize that climate change was very serious?

It was around 2003, when George Bush was in power and the USA refused to join the Kyoto Protocol. My trigger point was a documentary about the Gulf Stream. I spent so much of my childhood fishing off the rocks at Anglesey, which is an area very affected by the warm waters of the Gulf Stream. That is when I really started to get interested in climate change.

How does flying less affect your writing and your work?

I am on a train a lot, really. Most often I travel in Europe. I still do fly for work occasionally – and don't get too hung up on it – but not for holidays. Sometimes I just can't make the time – like when I flew to Germany a few months ago.

I don't want to want to be too heavy on the aviation industry. It's just a symptom of the whole crazy system. Some people want everything to be perfect before they agree to it; me, I just want things to move forward. Rather than being too negative, I'd want to work with the people who want to make fuel from algae or those working on communication systems for video conferencing. Then hopefully, in the future, flying will be a beautiful thing where a person saves up for the occasional flight fuelled by something that is not destructive.

How often do you fly now?

I turn down half the things I am invited to because I will not fly to them. I use Skype and the train. I do my best to stay out of the air, apart from a couple of absolutely necessary trips a year for work only.

What about flying to visit family what George Monbiot calls 'love miles'?

Many of my relatives went to Canada and Australia and only came back once or twice for the rest of their lives. That was the deal. That has changed a lot and it's very complicated now. My partner is Italian and flies home to her elderly mother every couple of months.

My decision to limit my flights creates tension in our house. It's a big thing to take that decision when others close to you are taking a different approach. The tension is worse around holiday time; my partner gets understandably pissed off that we are not going away to the sorts of places that everyone else is flying to.

In the big scheme of things, I know of course that my train trips make no difference to the global climate, just as being a vegetarian doesn't mean you expect meat-eating to stop tomorrow. But my main reason for taking this stance is so that when I am talking to people about climate change and they ask what I am personally doing about it, I can look them in the eye and tell them I'm trying.

What do you think of the youth thing … do they see it differently from the older generation?

For the older generation, flying is about luxury and leisure. I think that for the younger generation, who have grown up with relatively cheap air travel, flying is about freedom. You know – being part of a connected global culture, having friends on different continents, and having your friends view you as knowledgeable, progressive and able to talk about different countries and cultures – that sort of thing.

Right now though, because of the recession, the middle class is being squeezed and young people are actually finding it quite hard to afford even this relatively cheap air travel. So we may be in an interesting time of transition with that pressure. It is interesting to consider what the future might be. We are going to have to create something that replaces these feelings for the younger generation. Maybe we will have people limiting their scope and making more out of fewer travel experiences. I mean, if you mainly want to go somewhere exciting and hot [from the UK], Spain will do. Maybe that will be acceptable, without having to jet around to lots of other exotic places. Smaller travel hubs and a more communitarian approach might be the way things have to go. Maybe we will have modern-day pilgrimages where a student's gap year becomes this European multi-modal trip. Perhaps in a Magic Bus networked kind of way.

What do you think about environmentalists who fly all over the world?

It is really important how we talk about the issue of flying. Some very active environmentalists that I know have thought about this and decided that, since they are working on climate change all the time, flying is a necessary evil and something they are not going to get hung up on. The key thing is that you judge people by all their actions.

For young people, travel is big status symbol and a way to broaden their minds. People hear 'not flying' as a real attack on this freedom. The line of persuasion needs to be about the root causes of the issue. I realize that it will take people time to change their minds. This has to be about stewardship and new ways of living rather than a negative attack on air travel. I mean, I would love to fly more if sustainable fuels come on stream and that sort of thing, but that just doesn't look very likely.

There has been a real development in our understanding of how the mind works and how people make decisions. We know that they do not do so in anything like the rational way that we thought in the past. To me this has been a great error of the green movement, to think that by laying out facts and figures and hockey-stick graphs you will change behaviour. People don't work like that. We make decisions depending on who we identify with, what our friends do. It is vital that we have people standing up to offer another vision, saying optimistic things about progressive green politics. Optimism is contagious. People need to see a well-rounded person who they would be happy to have a beer with, and who can give them strong explanations for their stance on flying. That's why I think the examples of people like myself and others are important in order to show people the bigger problem, and to slowly reduce air travel as part of this move to a new way of living. We have to weave this into a new positive narrative. Otherwise you get the sort of thing that is current in the USA, where the right wing has cast all climate-change arguments as a threat to industrial supremacy and job creation.

The thing we have to address is this: if it's not going to be capitalism in the future, what will the new economy look like? Will people still have freedom to travel? Will markets work? There are lots of people working on this now, such as groups like the New Economics Foundation (NEF) and the World Development Movement (WDM) with their Plane Truths report on aviation (2008). Their ideas might seem radical now, but they are really very practical and worth taking a look at.

References

Monbiot, G. (2007). *Heat: How we can stop the planet burning.* London: Penguin.

NEF/WDM (2008). 'Plane truths: Do the economic arguments for aviation growth really fly?' Retrieved from www.wdm.org.uk/plane-truths-do-economic-arguments-aviation-growth-really-fly

4. Waking up to the downsides of flying

John Stewart

Photo © John Stewart

John Stewart has been an environmental campaigner for over 30 years, specialising in transport and noise. In 2008 he was voted by the *Independent on Sunday* as the UK's 'most effective environmentalist'. He is the author of *Why Noise Matters*, published in 2011 by Earthscan. He chaired the coalition that defeated plans for a third runway at London's Heathrow Airport. He chairs the UK Noise Association and for many years chaired the UK's leading transport NGO, the Campaign for Better Transport.

It all started on a beach on the remote Hebridean island of Barra. As a teenager in the late 1960s I stood by the water's edge with my school friend, rucksacks on our backs, as the islanders pushed and prodded the cows on the beach.

We were tingling with excitement. This was to be our first flight. The six-seater plane was about to take off from the beach to fly us home after two weeks' hitchhiking across the windswept islands that make up the Outer Hebrides, situated off the rugged west coast of northern Scotland.

I don't remember anything about the other passengers on the tiny plane. What I do recall is the sheer awe and wonder of looking down on the sea, the lochs, the hills and finally the sprawling mass of homes, factories and shipyards of industrial Glasgow.

It was another seven years before I flew again. I was accompanying a group of disabled adults who were going to London to compete in a national wheelchair dance competition. It was easier to fly. Ordinarily I would not have flown from Scotland to London. It was the 1970s. Flying was too expensive as a regular means of travel. There were no cheap fares.

My third flight was over a decade later, in the late 1980s. I flew from London to Amsterdam for a week's holiday. I decided to fly after I had endured a long, long bus ride during my previous visit to the Netherlands some years earlier.

Even in the late 1980s I didn't think about the impact flying might be having on people or the planet. That only happened several years later, when I found myself living under the flight path to Heathrow. I hadn't moved to the flight path. I had lived in the same area of London for 15 years. I was 20 kilometres from the airport. But a change in landing procedures meant I now had a plane going over my flat once every 90 seconds, virtually throughout the day. I was living under a wall of sound. I soon began to think about the impacts of aviation!

A local group was formed to campaign against the noise. We later merged with the Heathrow Association for the Control of Aircraft Noise (HACAN), the long-standing residents' organization that represented people living closer to Heathrow. In 2000 I became chair of HACAN. We were soon faced with an even worse prospect: a third runway at Heathrow. Already there were nearly 480,000 flights coming over our heads every year. A third runway would have resulted in over 700,000. And if a third runway had been built, Heathrow would have become the biggest single emitter of carbon emissions (CO_2) in the UK. In successfully tackling the threat, we fought one of the most high-profile campaigns against airport expansion the world had ever seen. Not just local residents, but also environmentalists. *The Daily Telegraph* described it thus:

> The coalition assembled is extraordinarily wide. It runs from radical eco-warriors to middle-class mothers in west London, hedge-fund managers in Richmond, to pensioners and parents in Brentford. (14 January 2009)

Long before the campaign was in full swing, I had begun to understand the impact of aviation on climate change. It is responsible for about 5 per cent of CO_2 emissions worldwide. This means that, if the aviation industry were a country, it would be one of the top ten emitters in the world. It accounts for as much CO_2 as Canada and the UK put together, more than Japan, and just 1 per cent less than India, a nation of 1.2 billion people.

For me, the choice was easy. Given those climate statistics and my daily experience of living under a flight path, flying was something I wanted to do as little as possible. I decided never to fly on holiday again. I have not done so since my flight to Amsterdam in the late 1980s.

However, making my choice a reality as far as business was concerned was more difficult. There is an irony here. My 'business' is campaigning against airport expansion. My only trips abroad were to meet with other aviation campaigners.

Initially I did fly from London to meetings in places such as Frankfurt and Geneva. And then ... I discovered European night trains. I could leave London after lunch and have my breakfast the next morning halfway across Europe in Berlin or Barcelona. Moreover, as I began to criss-cross Europe by train, I started to realize how much work I could get done. Time on trains is productive time, particularly with mobile phones and computers. I made £5,000 on one journey between Paris and Strasbourg! It was a funding application I wrote to a trust fund to assist our campaign against the third runway.

There are other advantages of train travel. Check-in times are minimal. Punctuality is good. Invariably you arrive right in the heart of the city. Of course there can be drawbacks. I can remember a man who snored all night on the overnight sleeper to Edinburgh. And he claimed he had been married for 35 years! There was also the time my old body ached after the 25-hour train journey from Lisbon. And then there is the cost: that's the big drawback to train travel.

Of course business travel is much less price-sensitive than leisure travel. And given both the chance to work productively on a train and the hours lost in check-in times and delays at many airports, the overall cost to a business of an employee travelling by train may be less than flying.

Reducing overall costs is also the reason why many companies are using videoconferencing instead of flying their employees halfway round the world. Research published by the World Wildlife Fund (2011) suggests that, following the recession, businesses in the UK are making a permanent commitment to fly less and use videoconferencing more. Nearly all companies which have reduced their flying say it's possible to stay profitable and competitive while flying less.

The key findings of the report were that:

- 47 per cent of businesses have reduced the number of business flights they've taken in the past two years;
- 85 per cent of those that have cut their flying do not intend to return to 'business as usual' flying;

- 86 per cent are either reducing their carbon footprint from business travel or intend to do so; and
- 63 per cent of those that responded now have a policy in place to reduce business flights, or are intending to develop one.

The main benefits cited by UK businesses in the report on changing travel practices were cost savings and reduced carbon emissions, but these were quickly followed by the ability to work during travel disruptions, having fewer staff away from the office and greater staff productivity.

Governments could tip the balance even more firmly in favour of the alternatives if they were prepared to phase out the considerable tax breaks the aviation industry enjoys. In most countries aviation fuel is not taxed and aviation is exempt from VAT in the UK. Given the climate and noise costs of aviation, it would make economic sense to impose these taxes.

My younger friends in particular are amazed that I fly so little. I tell them that these days train – or ferry – is my preferred mode of transport for most of my journeys. And it would remain so, even if aircraft were clean and silent.

My most memorable journey by train was in 2007, when I travelled from London to Istanbul to attend an international noise conference. The journey exemplified all the pros – and some of the cons – of going by rail. The experience of travelling through more than half a dozen countries, each with its own customs and culture, is far richer than a bland flight from one anonymous airport to another. The slower pace of travel becomes a bonus rather than an irritation. I'll never forget the memorable day on the 8.30 a.m. train from Belgrade to Sofia. Travelling barely above the speed of a bicycle, I could pull down the window of my compartment and see, feel and almost touch the atmosphere of the Serbian villages we were chugging our way through. At the end of that trip, I came out of Sofia's main railway station, three hours late, on a dark Sunday evening to a city lacking both streetlights and pavements, clutching directions to my guest house in a language whose alphabet was distinctly different. But I have a wonderful memory of the city which, in the light of the following morning, turned out to be fascinating, friendly and full of charm.

Of course the slow train through Serbia is not an option for every business appointment. But what my train journey to the three-day conference in Istanbul taught me is this: rail can be an alternative for the most surprising journeys. What it does require is a bit of planning. I arranged to take a few days holiday around the conference to allow me to break my train journey with nights in Sofia, Belgrade and Bucharest.

Careful planning means you can get as much work done when choosing the train as if you had travelled by plane. It does require you to get out of our current mindset. In 2008 I addressed a conference in London about rail travel. After my talk, a businessman stood up and said he could never have got to London from Edinburgh and back in one day without flying. As a busy chief executive, he couldn't afford more than one day out of the office. I asked him to describe his movements since he left his office the previous evening at 6.30 p.m. He told me he had had dinner with his wife, a quick look at his favourite golf magazine before retiring to bed in good time to catch his early morning flight to London. He checked a few emails and made a couple of urgent phone calls between the airport and the conference.

I put another scenario to him. Two hours' extra work in the office the previous evening, then a meal in downtown Edinburgh before catching the overnight sleeper to London. A few hours' work on the laptop before the conference and several more in the evening before catching the sleeper back in time for a 7 a.m. start in the office the next day. He acknowledged that this alternative scenario would have worked for him and admitted that it had never occurred to him to consider it.

This book is talking about flying less, not giving up flying altogether. My contention is that it is possible for even the busiest businessperson to fly less without affecting their productivity. It requires, though, this different mindset. We need to think more creatively in order to make it happen. We, in the Western world, have become so programmed into automatically booking a flight for a business trip that we have closed our minds to alternatives. We are almost literally on autopilot.

For me, flying less has required more advance planning, more flexible working hours, and the attempted mastery of computer technology. Of course there are times when I will fly. Recently I flew to Madrid for a conference: a combination of factors virtually ruled out the rail alternative.

Next month I shall be taking my first-ever transatlantic flight. I am going to take part in a month-long tour of the USA, speaking about the successful campaign to stop a third runway at Heathrow. I will be flying from Heathrow to New York. It will take seven and a half hours and cost around £500 return. The trip by ship would have taken six to ten days and cost over £4,000 return. Of course, if there were more of a market for sailing, the price would fall and passengers would no longer need to rely on either cargo ships or cruise liners to get across. Ships, of course, are not pollution-free. They emit a lot of CO_2 and are the main cause of noise pollution in our oceans, where noise levels have doubled every decade over the past 50 years.

The lesson for me from this is that long-distance travel per se, particularly by plane, ship or car, is highly polluting. It becomes difficult to justify regular long-distance trips. I've got friends who have flown to another continent to go to a wedding. I couldn't justify that. Perhaps the message to the bride and groom should be not to send out intercontinental invitations!

This behaviour is largely a feature of the Western world. Only 5 per cent of the world's population has ever flown. Flying is still a rich person's pastime. Poor people in poor countries don't do it. Yet these are the very communities that will be hit first, and most acutely, by climate change.

Of course, as people in the industrializing countries become richer, they will want to fly more. To give them some space to do so, we need to fly less. The aviation industry admits that new technology to cut emissions and noise will be offset by the number of aircraft in the sky if the growth of aviation occurs at the forecast rate in both the industrialized and industrializing world (Ollerhead and Sharp, 2001).

It is worrying that the industrializing world is trying to copy the pattern of mobility that is current in the industrialized world, where the mindset is to fly first and think of other ways of doing business second. That habit will not be turned around without deep structural and fiscal changes. But the mentality the habit has produced can be changed.

When I am in the USA I shall be criss-crossing the country by train. Train travel has been built into the tour. I am positively looking forward to it. It will also be a great chance to see the country. The days and nights on the train between Chicago and Los Angeles will be an opportunity to catch up on emails, write articles, prepare presentations and do background reading. This is a different mindset from the one I had twenty-five years ago when I chose to fly to Amsterdam to avoid the overground journey by rail or coach. Mindsets can be changed.

I have never been back to the Hebridean island of Barra since I made my first flight from it over forty years ago. My school friend has been back. He went there by boat and I would do the same. Not primarily because the little plane which still lands on the beach is causing serious emissions problems. Not because there is any problem with aircraft noise in Barra (although there is at Glasgow airport, where it comes from). The main reason I would give the plane a miss is that the quality of the journey would be far better by train and boat.

Addendum

In 2011 John Stewart flew to and from the USA but was prevented by the US authorities from entering the country. They did not give a reason but it is thought it was because he was to address audiences about the successful campaign to stop a third runway at Heathrow. Ironically, having never made a transatlantic flight in his life, he made two within 24 hours!

References

Ollerhead, J. and Sharp, B. (2001). 'Computer model highlights the benefits of various noise reduction measures'. *ICAO Journal*, 56(4):18–19, 32–3.

World Wildlife Fund (2011). 'Moving on: Why flying less means more for business'. Retrieved from http://bit.ly/fiL4Et

5. Slow and low – the way to go: a systems view of travel emissions

Kevin Anderson

Photo © Kevin Anderson

Kevin Anderson is professor of Energy and Climate Change at Manchester University's School of Mechanical, Aerospace and Civil Engineering, where he leads the Tyndall Centre's energy- and emissions-related research. He regularly advises government and industry stakeholders, as well as contributing to wider public and policy forums on climate change.

Anderson completed an apprenticeship in the merchant navy and is now a chartered engineer and a fellow of the Institution of Mechanical Engineers. He has ten years' industrial experience, principally in the petrochemical industry. He is currently a non-executive director of Greenstone Carbon Management – a London-based company advising leading firms and public bodies on how to manage their carbon emissions – and is commissioner on the Welsh Assembly Government's Climate Change Committee.

This chapter originally appeared as a blog post on
www.kevinanderson.info.

When planning the journey from Broadbottom (UK) to Shanghai, and also since my return, I have frequently been asked about the associated emissions: 'I thought trains weren't much better than planes, what's the difference?' 'Was it worth the effort for whatever you saved?' 'How much difference was there in carbon emissions between the train and plane?'

On the face of it, these and many similar queries seem completely reasonable questions to ask. But, in my view, they miss the point, and without trying to be overly provocative (that's for later), I don't think they are so reasonable – particularly from the array of informed experts who asked them. So why do I think the questions are unreasonable – and what would I suggest as an alternative framing for assessing emissions from travel?

Analysis

The following blog-style analysis is a mix of provocation, parody and some different ways of thinking about emissions from our travel. I've tried to make a coherent case on the basis of argument, but some of the language may not be what you would typically find in an academic paper. Nonetheless, I stand by the well-intentioned thrust of the case and if anyone has any substantive disagreements I'd be pleased to hear them. It is intended to hold a mirror up to the climate-change community – and as with all mirrors, it can make for grim viewing. I know: I'm still a fit 36-year-old when I look in the mirror – but a less fit grey-haired 49-year-old bloke stares right back at me!

My concern about the questions I've been asked fall into three broad and related categories. They were asked by folk who work intimately on climate change as a system. But not one person asked a systems-level question such as, 'How are you going to compare the plane and train emissions?' or 'Have you thought about rebound?'

All the questions relegated climate change to technical, quantitative or efficiency issues – which tell us little about what we need to do.

Opportunity costs, rebound effect, carbon intensity of time, technical and financial lock-in/lock-out, early adoption, role models, diffusion, and so on, are all concepts the climate-change community should be familiar with. Asking emissions questions without direct or indirect recourse to any of these is, in my view, neither responsible nor reasonable.

Unreasonable reasonableness – another Rumsfeldian paradox

The first argument for my concluding that these reasonable questions aren't so reasonable relates to it being academics working on climate change (among others) who asked them. For the last decade, the language of climate change used in proposals for funding, research council calls, brochures and government documents has been awash with terms such as 'whole systems', 'systems thinking', 'interdisciplinary' and the like. Put us in a room and we'll expound eloquently the virtues of such approaches and say that if we're to tackle big issues like climate change, we have to think on a systems level. But as soon as there's something that can be narrowly and readily quantified, we're like moths to a flame: here's something familiar to our 2,000 years of reductionism, some knowledge – but without understanding. The great virtues of systems thinking that we were waxing lyrical about a few moments previously are cast aside in the mad scramble to get to the numbers. We know what to do with numbers and, as Lord Kelvin so persuasively put it, 'When you measure what you are speaking of and express it in numbers, you know that on which you are discoursing, but when you cannot measure it and express it in numbers, your knowledge is of a very meagre and unsatisfactory kind.' Well, I'm not sure this always holds, and when we do use numbers they have to be meaningful. Isolated numbers tell us little about the system and, worse, they can lead to decisions based only on the bit we can measure – when this may be worse than doing nothing or taking random action. At the very least the numbers have to be contextual.

So having made the argument that systems thinking requires some systems thinking itself, the following sections outline more precisely defined and technical matters that underpin my concern that the climate change community continues to take overly narrow views of systems-level issues. We ought to know better.

System saving no. 1: relative dimensions in distance, time and emissions

If we accept temperature as an adequate proxy for our various concerns about climate change, then we know we must stay below a 2–4°C increase in global temperature. Thus the climate is only really concerned with our cumulative emissions over a relatively short period of time – a period longer than the Broadbottom–Shanghai train journey, but stretching only about as far as 2020 for 2°C and (very approximately) 2030 for 4°C. (There is some maths behind this, linked to how high we are on the emissions curves, the real emission growth trend, realistic peaks and what carbon budget we've squandered already; see Anderson and Bows, 2010.)

Coming back to the train and its emissions relative to other transport modes: for a systems-level analysis, it's an adequate approximation (although erring in favour of aviation) to consider the CO_2 per passenger kilometre for planes, trains and automobiles to be similar. OK, alone in a sports car with your foot to the floor will be many times worse than being sardined into the relatively new aircraft of some low-cost airlines. Similarly, four people cosying up in a diesel hatchback will knock the socks off any scheduled airline (that is, have much lower CO_2 emissions). But put a couple of academics in a typical diesel saloon car and any disparity in emissions between the modes over the same distance will be lost in the system noise. The difference, of course, arises from the distance we deem reasonable to travel – and really this is less about the distance and more about the time.

Attending an 'essential' conference to save the world from climate change in Venice, Cancun or some other holiday resort is perfectly doable by plane. However, emission trends don't seem to have registered the sterling work we have done at such events. Perhaps if we flew to more of them, emissions would really start to come down – we may even spot some flying pigs en route. Instead, junk the plane and get together with a few other UK speakers heading to the same event, cram yourself into a trusty hatchback and set off for Venice. Somewhere around Dartford, what was previously 'essential' begins to take on a different hue, and by Dover a whole new meaning has evolved. Essential has become a relative term, dependent on: Can we get there by plane? Are our friends also attending? Is it somewhere nice to visit (or name-drop)? Will we be taxied around? Are we staying in a nice hotel?

This is where the first major saving resides: slow forms of travel fundamentally change our perception of the essential. We consequently travel less (at least in distance), and given that air travel is the most emission-profligate activity per hour (short of Formula One and space tourism), the emission-related opportunity costs are knocked into a cocked hat. Of course, as climate-change specialists we are exempt from such analysis – our message truly is essential – so we're the exception that should be able to carry on as before.

Ah, yes, and business folk – we need them to drive the economy. Tourists – another really important economic driver (not to mention the great cultural gains from staying in Western-style hotels with like-minded folk and observing other cultures pass by the windscreens of our taxis). Next, there are the pop stars and celebrities – the world would be such a dull place if they weren't able to prance about at some international festival or other. The football and tennis players must test their mettle in the international arena – and of course they need their fans to cheer them on.

We can then turn to whole industrial sectors which put forward an equally bewildering array of 'reasons' why they should be the exceptions and exempt from major emission reductions. This includes government departments, climate-change think tanks and some NGOs – with the remaining less-deserving sectors and individuals taking up the slack. It really is a puzzler as to why emissions keep on rising – all the more so since fuel prices have rocketed to levels way in excess of any carbon price economists previously told us would collapse the economy! Still, a few more international conferences and guidance from the carbon-market gurus will have us turn the corner on this one, I'm sure.

Obviously these caricatures are so far from reality that we don't recognize ourselves in any of them – but nevertheless the message is clear. Travelling slowly forces us to travel much less, to be much more selective in what events we attend, and to endeavour to get more out of those trips we do take. Fewer trips and potentially longer stays: not rocket science – just climate change basics.

System saving no. 2: iteration, adaptive capacity and indulgences – how to avoid carbon lock-in

It may be apocryphal, but I have heard from several reputable sources that China is in the process of constructing 150 new international airports. You may think that sounds implausible, but China's population is approximately 22 times the UK's, and the UK has around 25 international airports (550 airports would be the China per capita equivalent of the UK). Suddenly this seems less implausible. Either way, flying to Shanghai sends a very clear market signal: expand your airport. That is exactly what they're doing right now, so they're reading our repeated signal loud and clear.

You may ask how that is worse than expanding the rail network. First, there is potential to radically improve the efficiency of train travel – until very recently efficiency has not been a major concern for the industry. This is not the case for aviation. Jet engines and current plane designs have pushed the orthodox design envelope about as far as it can go – so 1–2 per cent per annum improvement is about as much as you can wring out of the aviation industry in the short to medium term. In the longer term things may change, but not within the scarce time 'resource' associated with climate change. So flying now locks the future into high-carbon aviation infrastructure. By contrast, trains have substantial efficiency potential (though this may be compromised with the very high-speed trains) and, more significantly, trains can run on electricity (many already do) and electricity can be low-carbon (some of it already is). Trains can also have regenerative breaking (tricky with aircraft) and overnight trains can be used to flatten demand curves (and cut back on hotel emissions). Planes are currently locked into high-carbon kerosene, while trains already have several low-carbon options.

Jump on a plane and you send a signal that says: please buy some more aircraft that will have a 20–30-year operating life and a design life of typically around forty years; please build some more airports; please divert your public transport funding to ensure that I can travel from the centre of the nearby city to the airport in a low-carbon manner (before leaping on the pinnacle of humankind's carbon-emitting ingenuity); please expand the car park; and please ensure we keep seeking out the black stuff – because without it we will have invested billions on an industry dependent on kerosene. Lock-in par excellence. They don't tell you all this on the back of the ticket – though there may be some oh-so-useful advice on carbon offsetting. Again, is it any wonder that emissions aren't coming down when we can buy indulgences so easily and cheaply?

System saving no. 3a: opportunity costs – cost carbon

Here we turn to the old chestnut, opportunity costs. Basically, if I had flown (and assuming the direct emissions per capita were approximately the same between the plane and the Trans-Siberian Express) then what would I have been doing for the time I wasn't on the train? Let's say the plane took two days – one day each way (UK to Shanghai) – while the train took a total of 20 days – 10 each way – leaving an opportunity-cost period of 18 days. If at home, I certainly would have been taking the train in and out to work each day. I'd probably have had around four longer UK trips – typically at around 650 km (400 miles) per return trip. I'd have visited a few rock-climbing venues in my immediate vicinity around the Peak District (say 200–300 km (120-190 miles) in total, probably shared with a couple of others in the car); I'd have watched a few movies, listened to the radio a lot – and all the usual stuff. The total distance travelled would be equivalent to 3,000–5,000 km (2000-3000 miles) – that is, very roughly 10–20 per cent of the Trans-Siberian. But if I were a regular flyer, in the 18 days I would otherwise have been on the train, I might have taken a further flight or two, and if I were one of 'the great and the good' this would likely have been business or first class (with accompanying higher emissions). Add all this together and (if we treat offsetting with the disdain it deserves) the emissions from these 'opportunity-cost' activities could easily have exceeded those from the full return journey to China by train. And if offsetting had been used, I take the view that the emissions would have been still higher. Offsetting provides a reduced incentive for the person purchasing the offsets to change their behaviour, thereby increasing lock-in to high-carbon infrastructures (e.g. building new UK airports and purchasing more kerosene-based aircraft to facilitate 'offset' flights). It also creates an economic multiplier effect in the nation receiving monies from the offset; increased development increases income that in poorer nations almost certainly increases absolute emissions (for more details see Anderson, 2012).

All of this assumes my 12 days actually in China produced roughly the same emissions per day as if I'd remained at home in the UK. This is probably not too unreasonable an assumption – though for those who consider it essential to expound their low-carbon message from exotic venues (i.e. involving yet more flying), the longer stay in China would have reduced their emissions still further. This slow-travel stuff really starts to notch up the carbon savings for those of us who travel a lot – particularly if it includes international travel.

System saving no. 3b: The slippery slope: thinking low-carbon engenders thinking low-carbon which engenders...

A final point worthy of a brief note: making the transition from fast to slower forms of long-distance travel may engender slower forms of travel elsewhere. Once we've made such a transition, it becomes more 'natural' to avoid taxis and instead to seek out the public transport, walking or cycling options we advocate for others. Taxis are another market signal for more roads. Jamming our bodies onto the Tube (or the Beijing subway), or waiting for the reliable late-night bus from Norwich station to the University of East Anglia, all give much lower carbon signals, especially if supported with the occasional letter, either chastising the London mayor for not doing more with tubes and local trains, or complimenting Norwich bus planners – or however we think admonishment and praise should be meted out.

So there you have it: my potted account as to why I think the climate-change community needs to put its own house in order before wagging its hypocritical finger at others or advocating low-carbon solutions to ministers that we simply wouldn't accept for ourselves.

Final thoughts: can slow travel be justified within a busy university life?

My guess is that a common retort to my ramblings will be, 'It's OK for him, I'm just far too busy to take such a long time off work, it's just not practical – I've got to live in the real world.' But the real world has us flying halfway around the world to give banal twenty-minute presentations to audiences who know what we're going to say. Even if our talks are riveting canters through the intellectual surf, are they really so important that we have to be there in person and in an instant before launching off to dispense our pearls of wisdom to another packed house in another exotic location? Isn't our situation emblematic of the problems (such as fast and self-important lives for the few, no time for thinking, reflection and humility) that we are abjectly failing to shed any light on?

My life is perhaps not as busy as some, but I still clock up a fair few work hours, have meetings to attend, admin to do and research to deliver on. The train was certainly not as simple to organize as a plane – though next time it would be much easier, and I wouldn't worry so much about getting everything perfect and having back-up plans in place. Long and unusual journeys inevitably take more planning, not least to ensure the time spent travelling can be productive. And in terms of cost, the reimbursement system is just not set up to support such journeys. You'll likely have to dip into your pocket because long train journeys typically cost more than taking to the air. Moreover, receipts don't come with purchases of strange foods from sellers on station platforms, odd bits of accommodation and obscure visas.

So what of the work you can do while travelling? I had planned and expected my many hours of mildly enforced confinement to provide a good working environment. But I wasn't prepared for what turned out to be the most productive period of my academic career, particularly on the return journey. During the outward trip, I read a range of papers and managed to write another on shipping and climate change. However, after spending 12 days in China, bombarded with fresh experiences, new ways of thinking and new information, the return journey was a wonderful opportunity to begin to make sense of it all, embedding much of it in a paper which a colleague and I had been working on for the past year. This was the first time I had actually put pen to paper with regard to that research. The train's ability to remove many of the choices that clutter my daily life gave me the seclusion and concentration I needed to set to work on what has proved a very challenging paper. By the time Moscow arrived, I had completed about 75 per cent of the writing; this would have taken another six months, had I flown to Shanghai.

From a productivity perspective, the 20-day train journey easily trumped the 2-day flight. Counter-intuitive perhaps, but I remain convinced that a carefully planned train journey not only delivers lower emissions by an order of magnitude, but facilitates the process of research in a way that universities and daily life simply can't match. Add to that the 'slower' ethos that such journeys engender, and I think there may be early signs of making a meaningful transition to a low-carbon future – or at least a bridging ethos – while we wait for the panacea of low-carbon technologies to become the norm.

Addendum

Among the wealth of responses to the original blog post, a recurrent theme was: 'I really can't see how those of us with young children could spend twenty days travelling when we could be with our family. Perhaps I should avoid any long-distance travel, as the emotional pull to return quickly is inevitably very strong.'

I certainly can empathize with the challenge of balancing multiple pulls on our time. Climate change is ultimately all about families and friends – but not just in the here and now.

If the science is broadly correct and the emissions trend continues, then we're heading for enormous change for many families, even in the short term. These families may not be ours. It is much more likely to be those who have not contributed to the problem, have little income and live in areas geographically more vulnerable to climate change impacts. So the choice is about whose family and friends matter most. We choose to fly back to be with our family as quickly as possible, so as not to be away for more than a few days. But the repercussions (not on a one-to-one basis perhaps) are for another family in another place to face losing their home, food and water shortages, social and community pressures, and wider conflicts – to put at risk the very fabric of their families and communities.

Moreover, reducing time away from our families by using fast and high-carbon travel also has longer term repercussions for our own children. Are we rushing back for the sake of our own families or for our individual engagement with our own families? This is a subtle, but I think important, distinction. Are we concerned about our families only while we're around to enjoy and benefit from them, or are we more altruistically concerned, regardless of our own immediate returns? When we're dead and buried, our children will likely still be here dealing with the legacy of our inaction today; do we discount future value at such a rate as always to favour those family activities that 'we' can join in with?

I'm not talking about this solely in an abstract manner; most of my immediate family have gone on to more ethereal activity, leaving me with an uncle in Australia who is getting on in years and not in great health. I last saw him in 2004 and have since stuck to the difficult decision not to return to visit him. OK, I may relent one day, but in the interim I've been unable to reconcile my desire to share family memories with a fine Aussie uncle with the fact that my visiting him jeopardises others' abilities to lead good lives with their families.

Life in a changing climate is awash with such thorny issues and tough decisions. To me the guiding principle (supported by the simple maths) is that those of us responsible for the lion's share of emissions are the same group that need to drive emissions down – and fast. Technology cannot deliver the low-carbon promised land in a timely manner – so the future is in our hands, our lifestyles, behaviours, practices and habits. If we are truly concerned about families – others, as well as our own (now and later) – then either the overseas trip is not quite so important as when we could readily hop on a jet – or the time away from our family is compensated for by the value of our message; the decisions have just got tougher. Of course, it could be that we are that shining example of an exception to the rule – preaching real mitigation to our parishioners 32,000 feet below.

References

Anderson, K. (2012). 'The inconvenient truth of carbon offsets'. *Nature,* 484(7392):7, available at http://kevinanderson.info/blog/wp-content/uploads/2013/02/The-inconvenient-truth-of-carbon-offsets-Pre-edit-version-.pdf

Anderson, K. and Bows, A. (2010). 'Beyond "dangerous" climate change: emission scenarios for a new world'. *Philosophical Transactions of the Royal Society Series A,* 369(1934): 20–44 (doi:10.1098/rsta.2010.0290)

Part 2
Business beyond flying

6. A green travel experiment

Chris Watson

Chris Watson preparing to fly a Grumman Traveller from Wellington District Aero Club in 1983 © Tony Gates

Chris Watson has a passion for flying. He held a private pilot's licence and flew light aircraft for several years. He has travelled extensively around the world, is interested in aircraft and enjoys watching the land from the air. He is an architect specialising in user-friendly buildings, a role which sometimes involves working with colleagues internationally. He co-edited an architectural textbook with 24 co-authors from around the world – a project which was completed entirely without flying.

Growing up in an airline family

My father was in the airline industry from the late 1950s until the early 1980s, so he saw the transition from propeller aircraft to the commercial jet airliners that eventually became affordable for many people in rich countries.

Up to the age of ten I was used to flying on two or three holidays each year to visit family, and was a proud member of the Qantas Junior V-Jet Club. On each flight I would ask the pilot to note flight details in my V-Jet Club logbook. When I was a teenager our family regularly flew within New Zealand for holidays and weekend skiing trips, and I was lucky enough to have two European holidays. By my early twenties we had taken six family holidays in Asia and I had my private pilot's licence. I saw every flight as an inherently valuable pursuit. I was impressed by the technical aspects of aviation, thrilled by the speed, amazed by the ever-changing views of the land, and in awe of Bernoulli's principle that describes a wing's ability to create lift. After receiving air traffic clearance to take off and applying power to reach an airspeed of 60 knots, I found it magical to pull back on the control column and become free of the ground.

Flight training in light aircraft and occasional cross-country trips around New Zealand were enormous fun. I loved the total concentration on managing the aircraft – flight control, scanning the way ahead, monitoring the instruments and weather, managing fuel, keeping a listening watch on the radio and navigating. My home town of Wellington is famous for its extreme winds so, as a pilot, I enjoyed final approach in gusty conditions. It was also fun taking friends for flights to explore the local region and further afield.

After establishing my architectural business in the early 1990s, it seemed natural to develop it with connections to international architectural research organizations, and so I flew to attend their conferences around the world.

Reading about climate change

In 1896, Svante Arrhenius calculated the effect of doubling atmospheric CO_2 to be an increase in surface temperature of 5–6°C. In an environmental physics class in 1979, I learned that the greenhouse effect was warming the planet, but I made no changes in my lifestyle. By around 2005, I was reading *Guardian Weekly* newspaper reports about climate change research and I jointly established www.FlyandPlant.com to offset aviation emissions through community reforestation projects. I soon abandoned that project after finding out that the CO_2 emitted from aircraft stays in the stratosphere, changing the climate for many decades regardless of any tree planting. While new forests eventually absorb carbon from the atmosphere, the process is too slow to prevent a positive feedback loop.

When I read a 4°C climate-change scenario described in *New Scientist* (Vince, 2009), I realized how serious climate change might be. The article featured a map showing most of the earth's mid-latitudes as uninhabitable. In broad terms, the authors posited that inhabitable land would be limited to Siberia, Scandinavia, Canada, Patagonia, New Zealand, Antarctica and a few other areas. Even if it is possible for civilisation to make such a migration, history suggests that it is likely to be accompanied by conflict, and secondary disruption in agriculture and disease would be inevitable. In 2010, research by the Hadley Centre of the British Meteorological Office showed that a 4°C temperature rise is likely and that it could cause substantial changes to the areas humans inhabit (Anderson and Bows, 2010). My understanding of the Intergovernmental Panel on Climate Change (IPCC) conference in Cancun is that all governments except Bolivia agreed to continue emitting sufficient carbon emissions to raise the temperature by an average of 3–4°C.

My green travel experiment

I started my 'green travel experiment' to find out how I could reduce emissions in accordance with IPCC-recommended proportions, and what the effect of this would be on my business and personal life. Below I have documented strategies I found useful to achieve sustainable connections with less flying, identified co-benefits and problems, and described any change in my appreciation of sustainable transport journeys. In the spirit of an experiment, this discussion is organized under the headings 'Situation', 'Aim', 'Method', 'Results', 'Discussion' and 'Conclusion'.

Situation

In the last couple of decades, air passengers may have noticed green initiatives such as hybrid taxis, recycling bins and solar panels at airports, and winglets and LED lights in aircraft. These initiatives may have allowed some passengers to feel better about polluting the stratosphere. Aircraft efficiency has improved at around 2 per cent per year, but so many more passengers have been flying so much further that emissions have increased despite the 1992 Rio de Janeiro UN Conference on Environment and Development, and IPCC reports.

Airlines are using lighter aircraft on more direct flight paths, but have failed to make the substantial carbon emission reductions that are necessary for them to play their part in stabilizing the climate. If the airline industry were serious about efficiency, it would have been flying by the most efficient routes between airports for some years. But the industry's interest in fuel efficiency in the two decades since Rio has not yet been sufficient to motivate them to improve on a load factor which is around 80 per cent. If passengers were organized to occupy the empty seats available in aircraft, then up to one in five flights might be unnecessary.

The IPCC research found that six to nine billion people will have to emit less than an average of 1 to 2 tonnes of carbon dioxide equivalent (CO_2-e) per person per year over the next 50 years to have some chance of maintaining a habitable climate. Therefore travellers need to reduce air travel dramatically now. I set out to see how this could be done on a personal basis.

As a result of my interest in flying, I was somewhat sensitised to comments about air travel and noticed that people had an incredibly low threshold for complaining about it. It was as if they exaggerated the imperfections of air travel. They even derided their own choice of 'cattle class' (economy), despite air travel being cheaper, faster and more comfortable than most alternatives now and throughout human history. They suffered the indignity of body searches by airport staff, airport fees, parking problems, check-in queues, baggage issues, flight delays, airline food and close confinement with fellow passengers.

For New Zealand, outbound travel is a substantial cost on the local economy. Dr Yigit Saglam of the School of Economics at Victoria University of Wellington cites data from Statistics New Zealand which shows that 4.4 million New Zealanders take 2.1 million overseas trips every year (private paper, 12 April 2012). About 20 per cent of trips are for business purposes. Emissions are around 5.5 million tonnes of CO_2-e and airfares are estimated at around NZ$2.5 billion. If more New Zealanders 'staycationed' in their own country, money spent on international airfares, hotels, meals and other travel expenses would instead be spent within the local economy.

Aim

The aim of my green experiment was to test how I could lower my carbon dioxide emissions from both personal and business travel while maintaining a good lifestyle and a profitable business.

Method

I adopted the following strategies in order to minimize carbon emissions while remaining connected with people around the globe.

Reduce air travel

Most people would agree that air ambulances justify the carbon emissions, but flying across the Atlantic for dinner is frivolous. Somewhere in the middle of this emission/benefit spectrum are the decisions people make about, for instance, flying from Stockholm to a holiday on the Mediterranean, from Mexico City to a business meeting in Japan, or from Cape Town to see grandchildren in Buenos Aires.

I carefully considered what travel was sufficiently valuable to justify emitting carbon dioxide. Flying from New Zealand to sustainable building conferences in Europe was hypocritical, so I chose to miss conferences in Europe from 2008 to 2012.

Fuel-efficient travel choices

I tried the following fuel-efficient modes of travel.

Bus. Between city centres up to 300 km apart, bus services can be faster, cheaper, more frequent and more pleasant than flying. Overnight bus journeys of 600-1,000 km (400-600 miles) can offer tolerable sleeping conditions and they save hotel costs. It is helpful to plan a shower, nap and luggage storage on arrival to make it practical to work through the day.

Train. Overnight trains offer safe, clean, comfortable sleeping and affordable travel. Such train services are a practical means of intercity travel in Europe and Asia. Most daytime trains are comfortable and offer reasonable conditions to work in.

Car. Car sharing offers a low-cost way to reduce individual emissions per person. Emission reductions can be further increased by choosing an economical car.

Ship. Cargo ship journeys are reported to be interesting and comfortable, and ships have plenty of baggage capacity. However, cost, speed and planning have deterred me from using them. Scheduled cruise ships are reported to emit more carbon than aircraft.

Efficient use of travel time

I try to use travel time productively, to work, relax or read aboard sustainable vehicles. Power for computers is available on some trains, ferries and buses, and connection to the internet is often available by cellular connection or wireless internet.

Planning more productive trips

Well-planned travel achieves several benefits from each journey. For example, multiple business meetings or visiting friends and family during a single trip, rather than taking separate trips, can save time and reduce carbon emissions.

Innovation to avoid travel

Much of my architectural work involves minimizing the environmental impact associated with buildings. Architectural conferences and professional meetings are dominated by discussion about how to minimize carbon emissions. It seems ironic that so many people should fly around the world to talk about reducing carbon emissions in buildings. I calculated that the delegates who attended the 2005 Environment Design Research Association (EDRA) conference in Vancouver travelled an average of 7,000 km each. Like many organizations, EDRA does not offer videoconferencing for members whose mobility is limited by carbon, money, time or medical conditions.

Travel examples
Example 1: conferences without flying

Conferences typically attract people from a wide area, thus they are very carbon-intensive activities. High-speed internet technology makes conferences easy and cheap to attend, as was demonstrated by Susan Krumdieck when she organized the Signs of Change conference in 2010 (see chapter 9). From my perspective as a conference delegate, teleconferencing has both advantages and disadvantages over conventional conferencing. It doesn't allow the networking opportunities of meeting conference delegates, but it is possible to attend more conferences around the world online and therefore you can make contact with more specialists.

Example 2: ferry, train and bus replace flying

I wrote a trip report on a 1,000 km (600 mile) business trip. The trip used fuel-efficient modes of travel (train, bus and ferry) and I used the trip to visit family. The ferry, train and bus trip produced 32 kg CO_2-e, which is just 20 per cent of the emissions flying would have produced.

Example 3: sustainable travel with a teenager

In 2011 I took my 15-year-old daughter on a 600 km (400 mile) trip to inspect the building failures evident after the Christchurch earthquake. My daughter would have preferred the 40-minute flight to the 11-hour ferry and bus trip, but she accepted the journey. She suffered mild seasickness, but she was pleased to drive a car for part of the journey, since she was preparing for her driving test. Our travel emitted approximately 40 per cent less carbon than if we had flown.

Example 4: car sharing and bus replace flying

On a 2010 business trip of 1,200 km (750 miles), from Wellington to Auckland return, I shared a car on the outbound journey and attended two meetings en route. On the return journey, I efficiently used travel time to sleep on the overnight bus. This trip emitted just 12 per cent of the carbon that flying would have produced.

Example 5: co-writing books online

This book is an internet collaboration. I invited authors to participate by email and we collaborated online to produce and edit chapters. My previous book, on architectural evaluation, was produced using Voice over Internet Protocol (VoIP) calls and email. I have also accepted an invitation to collaborate online for a third book about architectural criticism and evaluation.

Example 6: less frequent long-distance trips

From around 2002 until 2008, I took annual business trips from New Zealand to Europe. This involved about 48 hours' flying and 8 tonnes of CO_2-e. From 2008 I declined to fly because of the environmental impact, but in mid-2012 I attended an architectural conference in Glasgow. It felt rather uncomfortable to read the 2012 *Guardian* reports about record summer Arctic melting that caused positive feedback from albedo, methane and hydrates. My intention had been to fly halfway and use the Trans-Siberian Express from Beijing to Europe. The nine-day journey would have reduced emissions by nearly half, but unfortunately visa applications for China, Mongolia, Russia and Belarus would have taken about a month to organize and required fixed travel dates.

The practical solution for future trans-Siberian travel would be to fix travel dates and apply for visas well in advance, then subsequently plan travel around the inflexible visa dates. By travelling an alternative route on the trans-Manchurian railway and through St Petersburg, it is possible to avoid the need for Mongolian and Belarusian visas.

Results

My personal (home) carbon impact is around 1 tonne per year according to the carbon calculator www.carbonzero.co.nz I achieved this by eating a plant-based diet, using public transport and minimizing the environmental impact of holidays. However, the figure excludes embodied energy in some goods and services purchased.

I estimate my annual business travel emissions to have reduced from more than 15 tonnes in 2002–8 to about 5 tonnes. It is not clear to me what effect the travel changes have had on my business. I have found convenience to be rather subjective because I derive some satisfaction from using sustainable travel and this helps me tolerate inconveniences, such as overnight buses. Sustainable travel is generally much cheaper than air travel and I can use most of my travel time productively.

Discussion

After four years of my green travel experiment, I have found many co-benefits of flying less. These are discussed briefly below.

Stimulating the sustainable transport industry

As a consumer, I prefer to buy tickets for more sustainable modes of transport rather than contribute to airlines' profitability. Furthermore, my decisions may influence the travel choices of my friends, family and business colleagues.

Travel distance = speed x time

Time cannot be created or destroyed, so it can be useful to maximise uninterrupted time in buses and trains to read, sleep, work on a laptop, relax, and so on. Car sharing with a colleague has provided valuable time for discussing issues in depth.

The 'miracle' of compound benefits

Financial investors talk about the miracle of compound interest to describe the exponential growth of a capital investment over time. Changes which cause compound savings in emissions can produce a substantial change in a person's total emissions; exactly what we need to stablise the climate. An example: I replace a third of my trips with teleconferences, reducing my total emissions to 66%. Then I combine a quarter of the remaining trips, which reduces their emissions by 75%, leading to an over-all reduction of 66% x 75% equals 50%. And then I use a train one way on each of the remaining trips, reducing their emissions by almost 50%; which brings me to a final reduction on my status quo emissions of 66% x 75% x 50% equals 25%. Reducing emissions to 25% of the previous year is substantial and it is rapid. This is the scale of change that scientists are saying is necessary to stabilize the climate.

Conclusion

The aim of my green experiment – to maintain geographically remote connections with minimal carbon-dioxide emissions – has been achieved. After five years, I can report that my annual travel emissions are down from more than 15 tonnes to about 5 tonnes CO_2-e. I have found several strategies to be useful in planning low-carbon travel and maintaining connections.

Once in the habit of using sustainable transport, I found it toler-able to use overnight buses and trains for journeys of around 600 km (400 miles). They are efficient in terms of time, cost and carbon, and they are sufficiently comfortable to allow some sleep and a full day of work on arrival. Shorter daytime journeys allow for productive reading and computer work, often with internet access, and can be as time-efficient as air travel when airport time is taken into account.

Teleconferencing offers the potential to replace much of the communication historically achieved with air travel. It has both advantages and disadvantages, which must be understood and accepted if it is to be used effectively. Substantial time savings from teleconferencing enable people to remain better connected with colleagues, friends and families.

Sustainable journeys are often more interesting than soulless airport shopping malls and aircraft cabins. Understanding sustainable travel options and observing landscapes and people's lives can make sustainable travel a richer experience at a more relaxed pace, with more time for friends and family.

I prefer to replace the airport check-in with a leisurely walk to the train station to begin my journey at a more relaxed tempo and with more connection with my surroundings.

References

Anderson, K. and Bows, A. (2010). 'Beyond "dangerous" climate change: emission scenarios for a new world'. *Philosophical Transactions of the Royal Society Series A,* 369(1934): 20–44 (doi:10.1098/rsta.2010.0290)

Vince, G. 'How to survive the coming century'. *New Scientist,* 25 February 2009. Retrieved from www.newscientist.com/article/mg20126971.700-how-to-survive-the-coming-century.html

7. Trains versus planes: building a low-carbon travel agency

Kate Andrews

Photo © Kate Andrews

Kate Andrews is co-founder of Loco2, a London-based start-up whose mission is to make booking a train in Europe as easy as booking a short-haul flight. She pledged to give up flying in 2005 and has since travelled around the world by land and sea. During a 26-month round-the-world trip she visited 31 countries and travelled some 50,000 km (31,000 miles) by cargo ship, bus, yacht and train, taking just two short flights. In this chapter she examines the barriers to a transformation of travel behaviours and possible ways to make flightless travel as accessible as airborne travel.

The environmental impact of aviation is difficult to ignore. Yet many of us choose to do just that, with the carbon consequences of flying remaining a blind spot even for many self-professed 'greens'. However, as one of the fastest growing contributors to greenhouse gases, and a major factor affecting the carbon foot-print of individuals, our dependence on airlines for even rela-tively short journeys is increasingly problematic. Emissions aside, the experience of flying lacks the thrill it once had. Journeys by plane are endured rather than savoured, with the destination infinitely more important than the journey. A diagnosis of modern air travel appears somewhat bleak: safe but soulless, a world of check-in queues, plastic cutlery and vacuum-packed meals served at your seat. Yet, even with rising costs, hidden extras and shoes-off security measures, most travellers continue to insist that flying is the only viable option, defending their right to fly with surprising vehemence.

There is, however, a movement of people looking for something more meaningful, who are shifting from short-haul aviation to slower, lower-carbon options. Could we be seeing a renaissance of the joy of travelling overland, of exploring, and of savouring the journey itself? Call it green, responsible or slow: call it a holiday! (When was it that 'going on holiday' became synony-mous with taking a flight?)

I'm part of that movement, having spent two years circumnavi-gating the world over land and sea to prove that other ways of travelling are not only possible, but more fun. It's not hard to convince people of that argument, yet the slow-travel move-ment remains a minority trend. So what is stopping more people from embracing the joy of travelling overland and shifting from planes to trains? And what needs to be done to catalyse change?

Around the world over land and sea

Faced with the convincing evidence of flying's contribution to climate change, I made the decision in 2005 to give it up. A victim of parental propaganda, my views on the environment were a hand-me-down from my parents. As a family we were definitely considered 'green', yet during my childhood we travelled to summer holiday destinations by plane and probably flew more than the average.

It was only later, realizing the extent of the damage that flying caused, that we switched from planes to trains, started holidaying closer to home and began exploring the places on our doorstep. Despite teenage tendencies to the contrary, I soon followed my parents' lead. It seemed logical. What use is buying organic, shopping locally and endlessly reducing, reusing and recycling when a single flight could undo all these efforts? That year I signed a flight pledge to abstain from flying for 12 months and spent the summer after graduation travelling by train around Europe.

That summer my decision not to fly wasn't a hardship. Having the freedom to hop on and off trains with an InterRail pass made me exempt from dealing with advance fares, booking horizons and the other manifold complications of international train travel. At the time I was blissfully ignorant of the convoluted systems that dissuaded others from travelling this way. It was only a year later, when I wanted to go to Nicaragua, that my decision to give up flying became less easy. And that was how, in August 2007, I found myself aboard a cargo ship bound for the Americas, with 6,000 tonnes of pineapples and 40 Russian sailors.

I spent the next two years travelling around the world. Having made it safely across the Atlantic, I lived and worked in Central America as a volunteer. Six months later I hitchhiked across the Pacific on a yacht, despite having no sailing experience. I found that once flying was taken out of the equation, incredible opportunities emerged. I earned my passage through Polynesia by cooking on boats, hosting pub quizzes and working as a deckhand. It was bliss. Sadly, it was almost impossible to get out of Australia without flying, so I swallowed my pride and flew to Singapore in 2009. I spent the next six months travelling through south-east Asia, Mongolia and Russia by every conceivable means, eventually returning to the Eurostar terminal in St Pancras to meet my teary-eyed family (who had never flown to visit me during my trip).

For me, travel means taking the time to appreciate the landscape and the view from a window seat, travelling through a country, not cruising above it at 30,000 ft (9,000 m). It probably goes without saying, but those two years were the most inspiring of my life. Before, during and after, everyone was impressed by my endeavour and expressed envy of the experiences I'd had. Yet I was surprised at how few people I'd met along the way doing something similar. Of course, not everyone has the luxury of taking two years out to work on boats and laze on tropical islands, but given the choice, not many would dispute the joy of these simple things. I'm sure that no one plans their summer holiday setting out to accelerate climate change. But the aviation industry has a firm grip on tourism, and for most people going on holiday really has become synonymous with flying. I've come to realize that until the alternatives can compete with planes in both price and ease of booking, travelling without flying will remain a minority trend.

The travel industry and climate change

In the last 20 years, global aviation and its contribution to greenhouse gas emissions has grown significantly. From 1989 to 2009 air traffic increased at an average rate of 4.4 per cent per year, and the industry is projected to increase by 4.8 per cent per year beyond 2030 (International Civil Aviation Organization, 2010). Despite vastly improved efficiency – according to *The Economist* (2006), aircraft today are about 70 per cent more efficient than those of 40 years ago – the savings are modest when compared with the rate of growth.

Admittedly, airlines have done a lot to reduce their environmental burden and a lower-carbon flight now means flying non-stop, in economy class, on modern aircraft with a high 'load factor'. EasyJet and Ryanair are among the most efficient planes in the air, filling an average of nine out of ten seats on each flight (Centre for Aviation, 2011).

The travel industry also tried to mitigate its environmental impact through carbon offsetting schemes. Such schemes spread rapidly in the early 2000s, indicating the number of climate-conscious air travellers, but in recent years the schemes have been widely discredited, exposing the disconnect between the aviation industry and efforts to protect our environment. In a sign of the times, Responsible Travel removed carbon offsetting from its website in 2009, and an industry of greenwash quickly fell apart as others followed suit (Responsibletravel.com, 2009). The exposure of 'carbon-neutral' flights, now deemed a 'dangerous distraction' (Bullock, Childs and Picken), demonstrated that there is no such thing as guilt-free air travel.

With offsetting widely discredited, airlines are coming under ever closer scrutiny from European policy makers. Aviation is now included in the European Union Emissions Trading Scheme, and the European Community is beginning investigations into the subsidies paid to airlines (Topham, 2012).

Few people are prepared to give up their freedom to travel by air, but the uncomfortable truth is that the only way to reduce aviation emissions significantly is to fly much less or even not at all. But while it's important to expose the continued and growing carbon impact of the airline industry, and to acknowledge the obvious need to regulate its emissions effectively, what's really missing from the debate is a comprehensive approach to fostering viable, lower-carbon alternatives such as trains.

Significant investment in rail means that the reach, speed and frequency of high-speed trains in Europe are impressive. Journey times are shorter than most people imagine, and the electrification of railways across the Continent means that trains are among the most environmentally friendly means of transport (International Union of Railways, 2012). Although the European rail network is a shining example of what a sustainable transport infrastructure should look like, passenger numbers are much smaller than airlines. So the question is, why don't more people go by train? Ask anyone familiar with travelling by rail and they will tell you that prices are too high and booking too complex. Without addressing these important points and embarking on a robust analysis of where trains could capture market share from airlines, the problem is only half-solved.

Eurostar: a success story

Eurostar is a blueprint for how high-speed rail can capture market share from airlines and keep planes grounded. Since its launch in 1994, the service has enabled a shift from planes to trains on a scale that should thrill environmentalists and train geeks alike.

Few people could have imagined Eurostar before it was built, but now Europeans can hardly imagine life without it. The numbers speak for themselves: a report released in 2011 revealed that Eurostar now owns some 80 per cent of the market share of travellers between London, Paris and Brussels (Eurostar, 2011). Not only that, it has increased the size of the market itself, from seven million to close to ten million passengers.

The London–Paris and London–Brussels routes have proved so popular (and competitive on price and journey duration) that few airlines continue to fly the routes. During the period of a ten year study of intermodal competition, 'two aviation alternatives exited the market [and] British Airways and Air France reduced their flights dramatically in 2009 and 2008' (Behrens and Pels, 2012), while Eurostar increased the frequency of its service. Faced with stiff competition from trains, only the most frugal operators can afford to stay in the race, and they persevere at the expense of passenger comfort.

Eurostar is just one of many examples of high-speed rail competing with aviation on speed and convenience. The route between Paris and Brussels, which operates two direct trains per hour – covering 257 km (160 miles) in 80 minutes – has effectively obliterated the market for air travel between these cities. The extension of High Speed 1 in the UK will accelerate the growth and speed of journeys between London and Frankfurt via Cologne, Brussels and Lille (High Speed 1). And there are countless other examples.

But where there is progress in the infrastructure and technology of high-speed trains, there are still significant market barriers preventing wider adoption, the most important of which are price and ease of booking.

Closing the price gap

The rail industry has a long way to go before it can compete with the marketing arsenal of airlines. The low prices offered by airlines are hard to resist, and the ease of booking impressive. Competition between low-cost airlines, and subsidies from governments that have ploughed billions of euros into the aviation industry (Emirates, 2012), combine to keep prices low. Even with additional costs tacked on to the advertised fares, flying is astonishingly cheap.

However, current budget prices are artificially low, and the cost of flying is increasing. This is due not only to higher fuel prices, but increased air passenger duty, higher airport charges to cover heightened security procedures, and legislative changes such as the EU Emissions Trading Scheme. The leaders of the low-cost airline pack, Ryanair and EasyJet, reported losses for the first time in 2011, blaming high fuel costs (BBC News, 2011). Airlines have cut every conceivable corner, but they can't shield passengers for ever from the true cost of flying.

As prices go up, so too do expectations, and this is where train travel can outshine its rivals. It's a frequently touted argument, but holidays by rail really do start as soon as you climb aboard. And for business travellers (or others not interested in gazing out of the window) the comfort and convenience of trains – with plug-in sockets and on-board Wi-Fi – is clearly superior to air travel. These benefits can justify a slight discrepancy in price, but the current chasm is substantial enough to ensure the majority of travellers won't change their habits. What is required is an economic transformation and greater competition between rail companies, in order that they can compete en masse with aviation.

One important way that the gap can be closed is by improving the provision for online booking. Here, rail operators can learn from the airline industry to overcome market barriers. Currently there is no robust system for planning and booking international travel without flying; train travellers will tell you that booking anything more than the simplest of journeys is a complicated process involving multiple websites, languages and currencies (and as a result, more often than not, customers don't realize that they are paying above the odds). When you compare this to vast, comprehensive online-booking airline websites such as Expedia and Sky-scanner, it's no wonder that more people aren't going by train.

And that is how we came to found Loco2. At the moment, train travel is considered a luxury, for those who can afford it and who have the patience to do battle with convoluted booking systems to find reasonably priced tickets. Our mission, to make booking a train in Europe as easy as booking a flight, means we are dedicated to helping train travellers find good value alternatives to flying. The digital age provides a fantastic opportunity for innovations in technology that can mount a credible challenge to airlines and catalyse a modal shift from planes to trains.

Regulation seems to be on our side, with the EU moving to open the market to competition, and encourage greater interoperability between rail providers. As boring as it may sound, a lot of the route planning and booking difficulties come down to the question of data. In order for up-and-coming businesses to develop new and better technologies, rail companies must cooperate, and open their systems up to innovation. Granting access to information, including timetable and price data, will accelerate efforts to make booking trains easier.

Properly realized, e-ticketing and innovations in booking will have a real impact on the environmental footprint of the travel industry. Getting people off planes and onto trains is a guaranteed way to cut emissions, in a way that offsetting never can. It's not enough to tout stories of low-carbon travel adventures without vastly better online booking tools for international train travel and proper consideration given to questions of price and time. We have to approach climate change as a challenge and an opportunity, one that demands practical solutions in the travel industry and all others. Flying will probably never be off the agenda and will be part of the future of travel. But it's no use getting up on a soapbox when the alternatives aren't competitive. That's why it's time that flightless travel got serious.

References

'EasyJet losses widen as fuel costs rise'. *BBC News Business*, 10 May 2011. Retrieved from www.bbc.co.uk/news/business-13343499

Behrens, C. and Pels, E. (2012). 'Intermodal competition in the London–Paris passenger market: High-speed rail and air transport'. *Journal of Urban Economics*, 71:278–88. Retrieved from http://bit.ly/wNBFcf

Bullock, S., Childs, M. and Picken, T. (n.d.). 'A dangerous distraction: Why offsetting is failing the climate and people'. Retrieved from http://bit.ly/Vtt2v.

Centre for Aviation (2011). 'European airline traffic and load factors up in Sep-2011, but outlook mixed for major carriers'. Retrieved from www.centreforaviation.com/analysis/european-airline-traffic-and-load-factors-up-in-sep-2011-but-outlook-mixed-for-major-carriers-60656

Emirates (2012). *Airlines and subsidy: our position.* Retrieved from www.emirates.com/english/images/Airlines%20and%20subsidy%20-%20our%20position%20new_tcm233-845771.pdf

Eurostar (2011). 'Eurostar contributes to rail renaissance as UK domestic passenger numbers hit highest level since 1920s'. Retrieved from http://bit.ly/IgmpMR

High Speed 1 (n.d.). 'International rail services'. Retrieved from http://highspeed1.co.uk/rail/international-rail-services

International Civil Aviation Organization (ICAO) (2010). *Environmental Report, 2010: Aviation and climate change.* Retrieved from www.icao.int/environmental-protection/Documents/Publications/ENV_Report_2010.pdf

International Union of Railways (2012). Railway Handbook 2012: *Energy consumption and CO_2 emissions.* Retrieved from www.uic.org/IMG/pdf/ieauic_energy_consumption_and_co2_emission_of_world_railway_sector.pdf

Responsibletravel.com (2009). 'Responsibletravel.com removes "dangerously distracting" carbon offset offering from its site'. Retrieved from http://bit.ly/gcrUOD

'The sky's the limit'. *The Economist*, 8 June 2006. Retrieved from www.economist.com/node/7033931

Topham, G., 'Ryanair hit by new EU inquiry'. *Guardian,* 4 April 2012. Retrieved from www.guardian.co.uk/business/2012/apr/04/ryanair-faces-eu-inquiry

8. Going cold turkey: a law practice without any flights

Tom Bennion

Photo © Tom Bennion

Tom Bennion is a lawyer specialising in environmental and public law, and indigenous land claim issues. Although he is active on many environmental issues, climate change only hit home at a personal level when he realized that he was reading books to his three young children about the wonders of coral reefs, but that they would almost certainly live in a world without them. His immediate reaction was to dress as an elephant and walk the streets of New Zealand's capital city, Wellington, to remind people of the 'elephant in the room'. He has been networking and writing about the issue ever since.

My earliest childhood memory is of sitting on my mother's knee, staring out of a plane window at the wet tarmac and smelling jet fuel. We were on a stop somewhere on the way to Ireland to visit relatives.

My other early memory related to flying is of a pilot's cap that my father gave me on his return from a trip to the USA to look at tunnelling machines for an 8 km (5 mile) rail tunnel through our geologically young country. Those were heady times. I still have a postcard he sent me from the USA, showing the Apollo 11 lunar module rising from the moon, and written on the back: 'Visited the NASA space centre, they were preparing for Apollo 12. Daddy.'

My first experiences of flying were associated with what we now call 'love miles'. My parents emigrated to New Zealand by passenger ship in the late 1950s. In their first decade here, personal contact with their family consisted of one telephone call at Christmas, pre-booked with the exchange, only 10 minutes long, and an occasion for much weeping as the personal impacts of events, such as births, deaths and other family dramas, were quickly relayed.

In the '60s and '70s, the rapid expansion and reduction in the price of aviation meant that by the time I was a child, airline trips to Ireland every half-decade or so were a family tradition. As for most people of my generation, domestic flying remained a rare bit of excitement in my early years, and overseas travel a huge adventure.

Holidays increasingly involved air travel. I made a Sydney-to-Auckland overnight return trip to surprise my mother on her seventieth birthday, and I flew to Dublin to surprise my brother on his fortieth birthday. Domestic air travel also gradually became a regular part of my work as a young lawyer, and international air travel for business was reasonably common for many of my peers. I remember remarking to my law office staff, not many years ago, about the ability to discover at 9.30 a.m. that I had a submission to deliver 600 km (400 miles) away in four hours' time, and, with internet booking and easy check-in, to make it there almost on time.

If one asks, 'Why do we fly?' the answers come tumbling out.

Flying is a great convenience, but I believe it is something more: a dream of freedom and power made personal for millions of global citizens. Someone else may be piloting the craft and telling you when you will arrive; there may be security hassles and economy seat frustrations; and you may get bored with it through overuse. But, for all that, reaching faraway places at such speed, watching the curve of the earth as you go and taking leaps that the gods would envy, alters us in a profound and exciting way. There is exhilaration, but there is a more enduring sense: we feel important, validated and connected.

So I have loved, absolutely loved, flying at such speeds. The technology is amazing. I still catch my breath seeing a jumbo jet, and the thought of an A380 super jumbo makes me smile. The journey – looking out of the window at sunrises and clouds, thinking about the miles rushing away below and the plane inching across the globe – has for me always been just as exciting as the destination.

Here is the statement which, in July 2009, stopped me flying:

> The Earth's atmospheric CO_2 level *must* be returned to less than 350 parts per million (ppm) to reverse this escalating ecological crisis and to 320ppm to ensure permanent planetary health. Actions to achieve this *must* be taken *urgently*. The commonly mooted best case target of 450ppm and a time frame reaching to 2050 will plunge the Earth into an environmental state that has not occurred in millions of years and from which there will be no recovery for coral reefs and for many other natural systems on which humanity depends. (Royal Society, 2009)

It is hard to convey terror in a scientific document, but I think the Royal Society in London managed it. The emphases are their own.

In terms of mass commercial travel by jet, the problem is simple. The aerospace engineers who brought us the moon landings developed 1,000 km/h (600 mph) mass transit, which involves taking large quantities of kerosene to high altitude and burning it. Had someone computed a reasonable growth factor and done the necessary maths in 1960 or 1969, they would have realized that this activity might become massive enough to amount to a crude form of climate engineering that might not necessarily end well. And so it has transpired.

We now know the numbers fairly well. First, air travel by jet is extremely intensive in terms of raw carbon produced. Carbon calculators show that an Auckland–London return trip generates around 3 tonnes of raw CO_2 per passenger. If you consider that one year of domestic car use produces about 2 tonnes, then more than an entire year's domestic emissions are generated within a 24–48-hour flight. Using the same calculators, an Auckland–Brisbane return flight (roughly equal to London–Athens) still produces around 0.4 tonnes.

Second, flight at high altitudes has a 'radiative forcing' problem. That is, it generates warming effects beyond the mere addition of more CO_2 to the atmosphere. This includes the fact that contrails consist of ice crystals that trap heat, further warming the earth beyond the raw CO_2 emitted. There are quite large uncertainties, but the Intergovernmental Panel on Climate Change report (Penner et al., 1999) suggests that raw CO_2 emissions should be multiplied by a factor of about 2.7. So those 3 tonnes of CO_2 are heading towards 9 equivalent tonnes, and even the return flight to Brisbane is around 1.2 equivalent tonnes.

Third, we know that the excess CO_2 we produce from flying is going to hang around in the atmosphere, warming the planet for a very long time: the effects will be largely irreversible for a thousand years (Solomon et al., 2009). To put this in perspective, the total planet-warming effect that the CO_2 produces over the thousand years it is in the atmosphere is about one hundred thousand times the initial chemical heat from the burning that produced it (Caldeira and Hoffert, 2002). Or, to put it another way: as you cross the globe by 747, the total warming effect of your flight is equivalent to one hundred thousand other 747s flying at the same time.

Fourth, emissions from air travel are growing rapidly. In 1999 the IPCC noted that civil aviation carbon emissions could rise by 600–900 per cent or more in the period 1992–2050 (Vedantham, 1999). In 2009, civil aviation emissions were already roughly 620 million tonnes of CO_2 per annum (International Air Transport Association, 2009).

There is no ready way to significantly reduce these emissions. The aerospace industry, which is our most highly advanced 'cutting edge' industry technologically, has looked at this from all angles, and the only way to achieve sizeable reductions, on a timetable to avoid catastrophe, is to use drop-in biofuels on the current fleets. There simply is no plan B. Sensible studies show that this is impossible on any significant scale, given the size and projected growth of the airline industry. And the impacts of climate change itself make it even less likely that ambitious targets for biofuel production can be met. As I write this chapter, the extreme drought and associated crop failures in the USA are creating political pressure to reduce the amount of land used to grow biofuels instead of food crops.

All of this means that air travel is the ultimate 'low-hanging fruit' in terms of a significant step that individuals can take immediately to prevent catastrophic climate change.

So, after the words of the Royal Society had sunk in, my reasons to stop flying were simple. The argument I might have with my wife – about whether it was right or wrong to take the kids to school in the car, or whether I should drive to work – made no sense if I was still flying. If I thought SUVs and Hummers were bad, what about that craft I was riding through the sky in on a fairly casual basis? What was more personally honest: knowing about the risk of catastrophic climate change but refusing to take the obvious step to reduce my largest personal contribution to it, or a sincere belief that there is no such risk? Real change does not happen without many individual instances of personal change. Those who drive big changes are motivated by sincere beliefs.

But I also realized that giving up flying represented something else that was important. It felt like grief. I was relinquishing a particular view of the world, my future and the future for my children, which a life of relatively unrestricted flying had given me. I would have to come to grips with a different way of life. That is why, on occasion, I still feel hesitant and embarrassed when I explain to people why I no longer take flights. After all, we consider fear of flying as a phobia so socially crippling that it requires treatment. And those I tell sometimes respond with embarrassment, or even on occasion feel personally affronted, as if my decision is challenging their world view.

These experiences of telling people have made me realize just how powerful the unspoken assumptions of our society can be. Fear of social embarrassment is a potent thing. But I also realized that fear of upsetting others would be a silly reason for refraining from taking action for my children – and seeing the planet warm by 4°C. I liken it to the reaction any parent would have if they saw an unsafe pedestrian crossing near their child's school. You don't wait for others to act, and you don't keep politely quiet about the danger.

Over time, seeing this reaction in others and observing my own hesitancy, I have come to think that a voluntary, drastic reduction in personal air travel is a kind of fault line for action in the climate-change debate. If seriously reducing flights is on someone's agenda, it lets you know they have got their head around how much we must change the way we live, how quickly, and what things we need to let go of – and indeed grieve over. The ability to get beyond our grief may be one of the biggest issues in the emerging crisis.

So what does this mean for running a business? Like all radical changes, it comes with challenges and some setbacks, but also positive surprises.

For me, the decision has mainly meant reorganizing work to limit the number of overland trips I make, because travelling by bus or train to a meeting several hundred kilometres away takes considerable time and energy. That has forced me to make better use of email, phone and Skype connections, and to make each visit to clients highly productive. In fact, I find that while I may have fewer client interactions, the meetings last longer and are more relaxed, because I am not rushing to catch a connecting flight.

I have had to give up the occasional piece of work, such as a land title case in the Pacific islands and an environmental case in the southern part of New Zealand that would have involved many long trips away from my young family.

It also means that I have had to become a kind of 'first-adopter' or revivalist for business travel, choosing transport services that business people don't often use in this country, such as trains, buses and ferries. I have had to work out how to travel long distances on overnight services or, if I travel through the day, work out which services offer the best power and internet connections. I have discovered, for example, that you can spend a very pleasant day at the office while taking in the sights of the country on a scenic train. I have become an inadvertent lobbyist for improving timetables, the quality and frequency of overnight services, and email facilities for overland travel. At the top of my wish list is a revived overnight sleeper-train service between Auckland and Wellington, two of our major cities. Easily achieved, it would allow business trips to be made within workday time frames not too different from flying.

Recently, I turned down an offer to speak in person at a university in the South Island just over 600 km (400 miles) away, due to the costs and time involved. I suggested that I appear by videoconference. That experience has led to other lectures. The university is surprised that for very little cost it can bring an experienced practitioner directly into the classroom at quite short notice. It is a good example of how my self-imposed change has forced myself and others into a new, more efficient and fruitful approach.

Has my choice not to fly been difficult? At times, yes, but it as not been nearly as bad as I feared. The hardest moments come when you have attended a meeting or a court hearing with your peers, and you watch them leave for planes that will have them back home within hours, while you face an overnight or longer journey. But there is immense personal satisfaction from the moments of insight that you gain, and from hearing of others who are contemplating or have already taken a similar step.

I believe that, because of the 'fault line' that flying represents in the climate issue, it would take only a few high-profile institutions (such as climate institutes at universities) and individuals (such as academics, politicians, or film or pop stars) to declare that their frequent-flying days are over, and we would have a whole new debate about urgency and what our governments need to do about reducing emissions. While many governments know that people want to talk about urgent measures to deal with climate change, they suspect they will be voted out if they institute the necessary CO_2 reduction measures. But people who have stopped or drastically reduced their flying are sending the message, 'We have the understanding, independence and resilience to deal with this. Now, what shall we do next?'

References

Caldeira, K. and Hoffert, M. I. (2002). *Warming from fossil fuels.* Retrieved from www.see.ed.ac.uk/~shs/Climate%20change/Data%20sources/Warming-burning.pdf.

International Air Transport Association (IATA) (2009). *A global approach to reducing aviation emissions: First stop: carbon-neutral growth from 2020.* Retrieved from www.iata.org/SiteCollectionDocuments/Documents/Global_Approach_Reducing_Emissions_251109web.pdf.

Penner, J. E. et al. (1999). *Aviation and the global atmosphere.* Retrieved from www.ipcc.ch/ipccreports/sres/aviation/index.php?idp=0.

Royal Society (2009). *The coral reef crisis: Scientific justification for critical CO_2 threshold levels of <350ppm.* Retrieved from www.carbonequity.info/PDFs/The-Coral-Reef-Crisis.pdf

Solomon, S. et al. (2009). *Irreversible climate change due to carbon dioxide emissions.* Retrieved from www.ncbi.nlm.nih.gov/pmc/articles/PMC2632717/

Vedantham, A. (1999). *Aviation and the global atmosphere: A special report of IPCC working groups I and III.* Retrieved from http://repository.upenn.edu/cgi/viewcontent.cgi?article=1066&context=library_papers

9. The no-flying conference: Signs of Change

Susan Krumdieck

Photo © Duncan Shaw-Brown, University of Canterbury campus photographer

Dr Susan Krumdieck is Associate Professor of Mechanical Engineering at the University of Canterbury in New Zealand, Director of the Advanced Energy and Materials System Lab, National President of Engineers for Social Responsibility, a member of the Royal Society of New Zealand Energy Panel in 2005 and head of the transition engineering firm EAST Research Consultants Ltd. Dr Krumdieck's research group develops engineering analysis and modelling tools to help transport and power providers to reduce their fossil fuel demand greatly – in other words, figuring out how to crash-land our carbon-based economy!

I couldn't believe that nobody had done this before! I wanted to organize a conference about emerging sustainability from across the spectrum of society. But I wanted to do it in a new way, using modern high–definition video links instead of travel. I wanted our conference participants to be able to 'walk the talk'. also wanted to allow more people to participate, as travel from the remote areas of New Zealand can be quite expensive. It turned out that my team and I had to design the networked e-conference ourselves, work with the computer technology geniuses to get it all set up and working, and take the plunge as the world's first 'no travel' national conference.

The Signs of Change national networked e-conference was held in November 2010 all over New Zealand. As the unsupportable nature of flying has become apparent, we need to work out new ways of staying globally and personally connected; this chapter showcases a successful step into that new future. Our experience has demonstrated that there is no reason why we can't take a huge bite out of our flying by holding conferences in the 'no travel' format. If I ever get the chance, I hope to make a pitch to a major conference hotel chain and conference-organizing company explaining how they could offer the choice of 'green' or 'beyond flying' conference organization to their clients. The results that we achieved in time and cost savings were amazing. This is what action on climate change looks like – better out-comes all around, by design.

The impacts of conferences

Conferences are a ubiquitous part of professional business, public service and academic work. The negative environmental impacts of conferences include emissions from travel and the higher energy and water use associated with hotel accommodation. The negative impacts for participants attending a conference include travel time, time away from family, and costs. The high green-house-gas emissions footprint of conference travel is particularly problematic for people working in the sustainability field.

The benefits for conference participants include time away from work to focus on a particular subject, learning from other experts, making connections and helping to advance knowledge in a field. The local economy also benefits from people coming to a conference and spending money on hospitality and sightseeing. There are also ancillary benefits if participants extend their conference travel to enjoy a holiday.

There has been little progress made in conducting low-impact conferences. The Signs of Change national e-conference was the first reported no-fly conference, and it was designed to provide the benefits of a conference while greatly reducing the negative impacts.

The Signs of Change model: how it worked

The technology to communicate via video link is well established. Communications companies can provide hardware, software and servers for corporate e-meetings, virtual presentations, document sharing and market presentations. The Yukon Room, Infinite Conferencing Media and Huawei are just a few examples of communications companies currently serving the corporate sector.

Universities and governments have tended to set up their own videoconferencing systems. In 2006 the New Zealand government funded the Kiwi Advanced Research and Education Network (KAREN) to facilitate communication between universities via dedicated e-meeting rooms. The Advanced Video Collaboration Centre (AVCC) was established to provide the IT services for the network, and in 2010 a new HD323 bridge was purchased to allow two-way high-quality video between lecture theatres.

Signs of Change was designed to be an electronically networked e-conference using a real-time feed of presentations between venues. A major objective for the conference design was to increase the participation of people from remote areas of the country. We also wanted to make sure that people did get together for the conference. Thus we organized conference venues in the main towns and cities of each region – basically the places where participants might otherwise drive to in order to catch the plane.

The conference had seven local venues throughout the country. Each venue was organized in the usual way with morning and afternoon tea breaks, catered lunches, name badges, programmes, vendors' stalls and conference dinners. The two remotest venues were at Kerikeri in the Far North District and Invercargill in Southland. These two venues received a live feed via a high-speed internet connection, but did not have interactive audio and video. The other five venues were lecture theatres at universities and the Royal Society of New Zealand (RSNZ) on the KAREN network. Each of these five venues hosted at least one session where all speakers presented from that node to the rest of the conference. Questions were also asked from the university nodes during the feedback sessions.

Getting around New Zealand: a good reason to fly or not to go

I realize that there are people who have taken a personal stand and decided to travel without flying. But New Zealand's geography poses difficulty with this approach. The alternatives to flying to the one central conference venue, Christchuch, are driving, regional bus and train. One of the main objectives of the conference was to reduce the travelling time for participants. The flight from Auckland to Christchurch takes 1 hour and 20 minutes. The odyssey by land would involve a 12-hour train journey between Auckland and Wellington, a 3-hour ferry crossing and a 5-hour train journey on to Christchurch. It is also likely, given the timing of the ferry and trains, that the participant would have to stop over for a night in Wellington along the way. There is no longer a passenger train from Invercargill or

Dunedin to Christchurch. The 80-minute flight from Invercargill would have to be substituted with a 10-hour scenic intercity bus ride. The most distant venue from Christchurch was Kerikeri. Two flights are required, with a total flight time of two hours and a brief 20-minute stop in Auckland. GoogleMap™ estimates that the distance is 1,310 km (810 miles) and the driving time is 18.5 hours. As this shows, holding the conference in one central venue would have entailed either flying or very long travel times. Using video technology to link conference venues across the country was really the only way to reduce both travel carbon emissions and travel time. The longest land journey to the Signs of Change conference was made by a registrant from Twizel, who travelled the four hours to Christchurch by motorcycle; and the only person who flew was one speaker, who travelled from Napier to Christchurch by air.

Organization: using less jet fuel means using more people power

A network of people in different cities was needed to manage the logistics of the multi-venue approach. Each venue had an associated group of people responsible for local organization and advertising. A major contribution was made by the participating universities and the RSNZ, which provided use of the lecture theatres, the HD323 bridge equipment, and full participation of the on-site IT personnel and the AVCC director, without charge. The registration fee for the two-day conference was kept as low as possible, with the professional rate under NZD $200 (£104) and retiree and student registration of less than half this rate.

Two system tests and one dry run were held in order to develop the plan for the conference. The technology performed in line with the high expectations during the conference. IT specialists were on duty at each venue to manage cameras, PowerPoint presentations, microphones and the bridge connection. There were no blips or interruptions in any of the connections, and participants were able to ignore the technology aspects and focus on the content of the presentations from around the country. Each venue had simultaneous two-screen projection, with one screen showing good-quality video and audio of the speaker and the other showing the speaker's PowerPoint presentation.

The national organizers handled all communication with presenters and registrants, catering contracts, collecting and receipting of registrations, organization of the schedule, and printing of the name badges and programmes. Local organizers, all of whom were affiliated with a university or the RSNZ, were charged with securing the local venue and providing local advertising and media relations. Local organizers also arranged any guest speakers for the local opening (before the network connection went live) and set up any local activities such as a conference dinner or breakfast discussion. During the conference, the main job of the local organizers was to act as moderators. They introduced speakers from their venues and ensured they kept to time. They also collected and asked questions during feedback sessions.

The run plan worked well and could act as a model for any future networked e-conferences. IT personnel brought the system live 15 minutes before local start times to test all connections and equipment. Local start times were set with an opening address 30 minutes before the national conference opening. This allowed time for each venue to introduce its organizers and audience members and address housekeeping matters, such as safety and emergency procedures, locations of facilities and food. The national opening was given a 15-minute time slot so that moderators at each venue could be introduced to the country as a whole and audience shots could be shared. The moderators also acknowledged some of the groups in attendance and shared local weather reports. This helped to provide an atmosphere of connection and a sense of each venue's identity. All venues held tea breaks and lunch at the same times. Sessions were organized by venue location rather than topic or theme. Having a whole session from one location made the moderation much smoother.

Management: overcoming the challenges of dead airspace

Keeping to the time schedule was seen as critical to the success of the networked conference format. Each venue had a moder-ator, a timekeeper and a communicator. The communicator was a person who had been involved in the organizational e-meetings and was familiar with the SCOPIA e-meeting system. The communicator had a laptop in live-chat connection with the communicators at all the other venues.

Questions and answers were a challenge for the networked e-conference format. It is essential that participants at a confer-ence can ask presenters questions. A new model was worked out through trial and error in the practice runs and e-meetings prior to the conference. Questions were put forward at the end of each session rather than after each individual presentation. At the beginning of each session, notepaper was handed out to par-ticipants. They were instructed to write questions or comments to presenters at any time and raise their hand to have the note picked up by a runner. The communicator would read the questions submitted and type them into the chat page. This way, all communicators at all venues knew what the questions were and which venue they came from.

The venue where the session was held moderated the question session. It was important that the moderators asked all the questions rather than allowing the participants to use the microphones. This was to manage the experience from the perspective of the networked venues. There would necessarily be time taken for people with questions to come to a microphone. This is acceptable if everyone is in one venue as people can see the person approaching the microphone and it is part of the process. But in the networked e-conference setting, these types of movements would not be seen by the other venues and would be experienced as 'dead airspace'. The question-and-answer process was organized to make sure dead airspace did not occur. The moderator would invite the appropriate speaker to come to the microphone, and then ask the question while the speaker approached. The speaker would then answer the question and possibly follow up with the moderator. The system worked well, and feedback from participants was positive.

The impact of Signs of Change

The impact of the Signs of Change networked e-conference can be examined in terms of travel time, cost savings and carbon emissions avoided. To do this, we compare the impacts of the e-conference with the calculated impacts of a non-e-conference of similar size. This calculation assumes that the conference was held in Christchurch and that all 176 participants who were not from Christchurch attended the conference by flying on the national carrier, Air New Zealand, and spent two nights in a hotel. The cost savings from using the networked e-conference are estimated to be more than NZ\$140,000 (£74,000) or, on average, NZ\$835 (£434) per person. This level of travel cost would have precluded many of the registrants from participating in the conference.

Carbon emissions were not objectively 'reduced' by the e-conference; the e-conference simply resulted in lower emissions than a standard-format conference. Carbon 'savings' were calculated using CarboNZero (see www.carbonzero.co.nz), and are not meant to represent an actual carbon reduction. The savings represent the difference between what was emitted and what a standard-format conference would have emitted. The carbon emissions associated with hotel nights and air travel for the standard-format conference would equal 86,671.58 kg CO_2-e (kilograms of carbon dioxide equivalent). In comparison, for the e-conference, where all the participants in other cities did not fly and stayed at their own homes, the associated carbon emissions were 84.48 kg CO_2-e. Thus, the carbon (and energy) intensity of the e-conference was 1,000 times lower than a normal conference.

The design of the Signs of Change national networked e-conference could be used for other national e-conferences. As an alternative to using universities as venues, a major hotel chain could establish the dedicated network and IT expertize required. The hotel could provide catering and IT services for the whole conference as a package. Conference organizers would also need to have more staff on the ground because of the multiple venues. If a hotel chain were to offer a no-fly conference, it would be prohibitively expensive to hire the venues at all locations at the standard rate. However, the size of each venue at the local conference venues could be smaller than if the conference were only held in one location. Given the savings in time and air travel, and possibly hotel nights, we believe that a higher price-point for a no-fly conference could be achieved.

The Signs of Change conference demonstrated the concept, design, technology and positive benefits of a no-fly, minimum-travel conference. It showed that people can have the connections and exchange of ideas at a fraction of the financial, time and carbon costs. Looking to the future, working with private-sector providers to develop business plans for no-fly conference services would help to make this model widely replicable across different countries and contexts, enabling greater connection and less flying.

References

Krumdieck, S. and Orchard, S. (2011), 'Signs of Change National Networked e-Conference: Highlighting emerging sustainability and social business', *Social Business* 1(1):37–58, available at www.westburn-publishers.com/social-business.

A documentary was made about the conference and can be viewed at www.signsofchange.org.nz/

10. Slowlier than thou: why flight-free travel is about better, not less

Ed Gillespie

Photo © Ed Gillespie

Ed Gillespie is co-founder of Futerra (www.futerra.co.uk), one of the world's leading specialist sustainability communications agencies. In 2007–8 he circumnavigated the globe without flying. A former marine biologist, Ed is passionate about the sea and slow travel, and he loves a trans-oceanic crossing on a cargo ship. Ed writes regularly for various media on sustainability and sits on the London Sustainable Development Commission. He is director of, and an investor in, www.loco2.com, which pioneers European rail travel as an alternative to short-haul flights. He dices with death daily in London on his trusty Dutch bicycle. You can follow him on Twitter: @frucool.

Flying makes the world seem small. But let's face it, it's not. It's a 40,000 km (25,000 mile) journey around the equator – that's a bit more than a stroll in the park. I went all the way around the world without flying in 2007–8, and let me assure you that when you bump across every last dusty mile of land from London to Singapore, toss on the crest of each briny wave of the Timor, Tasman and Pacific seas and oceans, rattle through Central America and blow back across the brooding Atlantic to Blighty, the world feels like a mighty big place!

Rapid, affordable aviation has opened up the world, meaning that it's possible for any idiot to twang themselves to the other side of the globe in around 24 hours. In some ways this connectivity has been great: creating the sense of a global village, fostering cultural understanding, opening our eyes to the great diversity of the human family and the wonders of the world, and of course enhancing international tourism and business markets. But it's worth also noting what we've lost: the sense of scale and adventure; the challenge of travel; the wonderful sense of transition that overland journeys involve; and the slow shifts in landscape, culture, people, language or cuisine that reveal the planet and its peoples' rich and varied delights. In some ways the swift, almost brutal experience of flight that whisks you from the cool, grey, urbane Heathrow in west London to hot, steamy, frenzied Chhatrapati Shivaji airport in Mumbai actually serves to reinforce perceived barriers and divides. Flying confronts us joltingly and jarringly with our differences, whereas flightless travel eases us more smoothly across and through those elements that might separate us. From topography to the way we talk, its grounded gradualism reveals far more about what connects us and what we all share.

The ongoing human obsession with ever-increasing speed also raises questions about our experience of travel. We have witnessed around two centuries of unimpeded acceleration since Stephenson's pioneering contraption *Rocket*, the first steam locomotive, took to the tracks in 1829. Almost constant innovation ever since, from coal to diesel to high-octane aviation fuel, through steam, combustion and jet engines, brought us to the pinnacle of supersonic passenger travel: Concorde. However, following Concorde's early retirement in 2003, we experienced a moment unheard of in over 170 years. Human travel just got slower.

Is this the end of progress? Well, hardly. In so many areas of bustling modern life the desire to slow down just a little is not only increasingly attractive, but also rewarding. Take food, for example. The supposedly inexorable trajectory of fast food should find us all fisting fodder as fuel frantically into our faces: a functional, efficient and effective way of cramming other more important things into our day. Yet we know this is not the case and that there is something special about a lovingly sourced and prepared home-cooked meal which is to be savoured in every sense of the word.

Travel is no different. Time is literally all we have in life. Paradoxically our response is to go at life harder and faster in the belief that this will mean we get more out of it. To some extent this might be true. But as Abraham Lincoln famously put it, 'In the end, it's not the years in your life that count. It's the life in your years.' In the travel sense it is therefore not about where we journey, but rather about how we do it. A wham-bam-thank-you-ma'am holiday or a cheap, quick, mechanically recovered meat burger may be forms of travel or food, but they're not quite the same experience as a long, slow-cooked, sensuous supper or a sinuous, scenic train journey.

Taoists understood this, their notion being that the journey, not the destination, is the reward. In life it's the experience along the way that matters, not the ultimate destination – which is, unfortunately, death. During my flightless circumnavigation of the planet, I joked that one had better hope the journey really was the reward, as the final destination was the point from which I'd set out and was likely to be a disappointment – unless, like me, you really, really like Brixton, London.

We seem to be entering an era of 'hypermobility', in which the idea is taking root that it is somehow our right to travel wherever, whenever and however often we want. It is fascinating to consider to what extent this is demand- or industry-led. The recent explosion in cheap short-haul flights from the UK to what were once relatively obscure east European cities is a case in point. It is unlikely there was an untapped latent demand or 'need' for UK stag parties to fly to Tallinn or Riga for drink and debauchery. Low-cost airlines deftly manufactured that desire through discounted pricing strategies.

It is important to explore the purpose of travel. A debate has long raged over how to differentiate between the idea of travel and the practice of tourism. I don't want to get into the smug and often snobbish semantics of 'tourists' versus 'travellers', though crudely speaking the most obvious distinction might be the relative focus on the destination as opposed to the journey, as outlined above. For me, it's more about 'it ain't what you do, it's the way that you do it'.

In this context the desire to escape your day-to-day life, maybe tan your pale buttocks on a beach and sip something cold, sweet and sticky by the sea is no less valuable or worthy than the urge to immerse yourself in local culture, travel like a 'native' or learn an obscure dialect. I'm not making value judgements here. But there is still such a thing as sustainability to consider, and I would argue that the sustainable holiday is simply the better holiday.

There is a parallel to the world of ethical investment in this. Many ethically and socially responsible funds outperform the stock market as a whole, simply because fund managers have to scrutinize their investments much more carefully in order to authenticate their ethics. As a result they know the businesses more intimately and thus have a better insight into their likely performance and success. They know they are better businesses.

Again, travel is no different. Even a package holiday that embraces sustainability is likely to be a much more satisfying experience if the accommodation has renewable energy systems, water conservation, local and seasonal food sourcing and so on, simply because these are all additional considerations that the business has undertaken. Greater consciousness and awareness of these environmental aspects, as well as social and economic factors such as the degree of local employment, engagement and inclusion in the commercial benefits of tourism, just make for a better vacation, full stop.

Why we travel is also changing. The travel industry tends to carve these reasons up into three basic categories: holidays, visiting friends and relatives, and business. According to the Health Protection Agency, in the last ten years there has been a big increase in visiting friends and relatives (+45 per cent since 2000), a stagnation in holidays (−0.5 per cent) and a significant decline in business travel (−25 per cent) (Health Protection Agency, 2012).

How important really is airport expansion to commerce, given the decline in business travel? There's a clear benefit to kicking off contracts face-to-face, but for ongoing relationships, video conferencing is now of good enough quality and is cheaper, less stressful and less tiring for the people involved. Organizations like World Wide Fund (WWF) encourage a 'fourth meeting rule' for business relationships, whereby after three 'flesh-pressing' personal meetings, chemistry is established and video-conferencing is both more than adequate and likely preferable for any further meetings. WWF's 'One in Five Challenge' asks businesses to commit to cutting their flights by 20 per cent in the next five years. They have so far achieved thousands of tonnes in carbon emissions savings through avoided flights, showing that businesses are able and willing to make this change.

Other businesses have offered 'social proof' that it's OK not to travel. Lloyds TSB's monthly 'No Travel Week' actively encourages employees to avoid all but essential travel for one week a month. During that week, video conferencing leaps by 40 per cent but there is little associated 'backdraft' (in other words, travel isn't simply displaced from 'No Travel Week' into the rest of the month). This initiative sends a strong signal that staff aren't expected to rush around like maniacs. As well as enhancing employee well-being, it also saves money and carbon to boot. Business travel is a declining, and already a minority, component of the reasons why we travel. In a carbon-constrained world of climate change and ever improving virtual-meeting technology, this trend is likely to continue. Hence punditry that suggests expanding airport capacity is crucial to the economy is both misguided and ill-informed.

Historically, flying has been about aspiration and prestige. It was glamorous and privileged to fly, whether for holidays to exotic destinations or because you were important enough to fly on international business. That has waned in the cattle-truck context of budget aviation and the singularly unglamorous experience of 'the red-eye' (even if now you get to lie down in business class).

In contrast, particularly with the extending high-speed rail network of Europe, the train is often now a classier, less stressful, more relaxing and productive way to travel. Yet the notion of a jet-set lifestyle is still deeply engrained as somehow cool. Visiting friends in Málaga, southern Spain, I argued that my journey was more in keeping with the idea of jet-setting: Eurostar London to Paris, drinks on the Seine with friends, eating a fine dinner on the sleeper train to Madrid, awakening as the first light illuminated the surrounding rocky plateau, breakfasting on coffee and pastries, strolling in the Retiro gardens before lunch, then the fast train to Málaga in the afternoon and dinner by the beach, with all the other interest of the places in between. Sure, it takes 24 hours and costs a little more, but it has a certain *je ne sais quoi* that the three-hour economy-class flight from London or Luton can't compete with.

Another challenge is that we don't compare like with like, whether it's time, cost or quality of experience. We usually compare travel times for train journeys from city centre to city centre with just the flight time of a journey by plane, ignoring the transit time to and from airports, the compulsory terminal loitering pre- and post-flight, and so on. The three-hour flight to Málaga is actually more like a seven-hour journey, all told.

But the biggest barriers to encouraging people to travel by train over plane are cost and logistics. Is it possible and affordable, and how do you do it? Again, cost comparisons between trains and planes are usually flawed. The price of a flight is wilfully deceptive in some cases, with a myriad of arcane hidden fees (for example, if you want to check in manually, have lost your boarding card or wish to actually carry luggage). This is even before you consider the massive financial advantage aviation enjoys in the absence of a fuel tax.

Almost everywhere in Europe is within a 24-hour train journey from London, but booking reasonably priced tickets is still a challenge due to multiple failures of train companies to integrate their booking systems. It's been left to genius amateur advocates like Mark Smith, the legendary 'Man in Seat 61', to bust myths and offer up-to-date and detailed 'how to' information on global rail travel. A former rail ticketing expert, Mark's website www. seat61.com is the go-to place for objective, informal advice on global rail travel. His expertize and enthusiasm have been rewarded by his website receiving well over half a million visitors a month. Similarly, the talented gang at Loco2 travel, a web business I have also personally invested in, have aimed at 'one-click' ticket-booking for transcontinental Europe train journeys, making rail trips as quick, simple and easy to book as cheap flights.

Of course, long-haul flights will always have a role to play. Not everyone can, or few would even want to, do as I did and spend seven months travelling over land and sea to Australia. Whilst I am optimistic in the long term that some sort of hyper-efficient techno-fix or genuinely sustainable alternative fuel will emerge for the aviation industry, the uncomfortable truth is that few of these large-scale decisive actions on climate change will likely be forthcoming by the time we need them – in the next ten years. Our only real option is flying smarter and perhaps emitting our precious carbon only for the types of flight for which there really are no practical alternatives.

I was lucky enough to fly in an airship over London a couple of years ago, a mode of transport that might have a small role to play in sustainable aviation, especially long haul, in the future. As the huge dirigible floated gently into the air from a grassy, green suburban field, I was struck by the serenity of its flight compared with the aggressive roar and thrust of a conventional jet engine. It's easy to forget that airships were once the height of flying fashion, flitting across the Atlantic in just three days in the 1930s. However, the horror of the Hindenburg crash in 1937, as its uplifting hydrogen exploded into flame, still lingers in the collective memory. Plus, the potential global shortage of helium (the safer alternative to the extremely flammable hydrogen) means airships are, sadly, likely to play only a minor role in the air passenger transport of tomorrow.

To avoid becoming ever more unsustainably 'hypermobile', we will have to travel less often but perhaps for longer stints. The five-yearly extended sabbatical from work may have to become the norm for which we save up our flights for an occasional three-month adventure, rather than expect to take two or more long-haul holidays a year or repeatedly bunny-hop off on short-haul 'city breaks'. Individuals and companies alike are going to have to think creatively about how and when holidays are taken. In this way I'm trying to 'walk the talk'. In the company I co-founded, a specialist sustainability communications agency called Futerra, we offer staff who 'slow travel' in Europe by train instead of plane an extra day of leave to compensate for the additional time supposedly 'lost' travelling overland. This formal Slow Travel Policy is proving a popular incentive for lower carbon holidays and 'traincations' among our team.

Perhaps the biggest challenge and opportunity, however, is changing our psychology and perceptions about what it really means to travel. The nineteenth-century philosopher Arthur Schopenhauer once said, 'The task is not so much to see what no one yet has seen, but to think what nobody yet has thought about that which everybody sees.' Real travel is therefore not about sights and checklists, or even discovering the unique experience on the road less travelled, but about a state of mind. In *The Art of Travel* (2003), modern philosopher Alain de Botton builds on this idea and suggests that we can achieve the same senses of escapism, excitement, intrigue, freedom or interest that we obtain from a holiday simply by consciously engaging in the familiar with the same open-eyed enthusiasm we adopt when travelling or as a tourist.

Inspired by this idea, I am also in the process of developing an interactive online and partly crowd-sourced website for London, provisionally and slightly sarcastically titled 'Air London'. So many of the brilliant aspects of travel (meeting people from different cultures who speak different languages and have different world views, music, art, cooking and dancing) are possible to experience without leaving a major metropolitan and multicultural city like London. 'Air London' will provide a dynamic listings service navigable via a world map that allows users to search for activities in relation to a particular country. Choose 'China', for example, and you'll obtain links for the best Chinese restaurants, galleries displaying Chinese art exhibitions (or museums with significant Chinese artefacts in their permanent collections), gigs by Chinese musicians, or historical and cultural sites from the obvious Chinatown through to the more discreet Fo Guang Shan Temple. Users can then collate their own Chinese itinerary for a deeply immersive, multi-sensory Chinese London experience right on their own doorstep. Many of the joys, thrills and spills of global travel, but without the carbon emissions and risk of deep-vein thrombosis!

My parents met during their early careers on a much more sedate form of transport, the cruise ship, working as stewards. Marine travel was the affordable way for their 1960s generation to see the world. Aviation has filled that gap for a new generation or two. But I do wonder how much its quantitative benefits in terms of time and cost will continue to outweigh its qualitative shortcomings with respect to climate change and relative richness of experience in the longer term. Is it just a conscious compromise between climate impact and cheap convenience – a carbon price worth paying? Or a matter of conscience?

My views have nothing to do with being 'anti-flying'. They are drawn from a cool-headed, dispassionate analysis of the impact of flying on my personal carbon footprint (it's the single most carbon-intensive activity or behaviour we as individuals can undertake – unless you perhaps habitually drive a tank to work). How flying fits into our personal collective climate-change challenge and where possible carbon efficiencies and solutions lie are the real issues.

While aviation's contributions to global carbon emissions are relatively minor, these are emissions caused largely voluntarily by a minority of people, many of whom are what might be called 'binge-flyers' – flying several times a year. Importantly, these few also set global aspirations. There are undoubtedly a far, far greater number of people who want to fly than actually can or are even likely to be able to do so, so there is an issue of climate equity here too. Denigrating this aspiration, attacking flying and criticising what most see as a natural, normal desire is, as many environmentalists such as Mark Lynas have pointed out, likely to create what psychologists call 'reactance': backlash and extreme defensiveness. Instead, I think that we must be 'pro-alternatives'. We must make smart substitutes, not sacrifice, avoiding creating a sense of loss or the idea that by not flying we are somehow missing out. In the eight years or so since I gave up flying on holiday (unavoidably I have had to fly on a couple of occasions for business in the last ten years), I have had an amazing time. I have travelled all over Europe by train from Sweden to Spain, Slovenia to Switzerland, been all the way around the world without going anywhere near a plane and, perhaps most importantly, realized that you can learn, appreciate and be inspired by the world without necessarily generating a climate-stewing slew of carbon emissions in the process. This is the joy of slow, low-carbon travel.

My journeys may be more grounded than those made cruising at 30,000 ft, but this does not mean my horizons are set any lower. The slower-travelling bandwagon is pulling languidly out of the station; there's still plenty of time to hop aboard.

References

De Btton, A. (2003). *The Art of Travel*. London: Penguin

Health Protection Agency (2012). 'Global and UK travel trends'. Retrieved from www.hpa.org.uk/webc/HPAwebFile/HPAweb_C/1317132797054

Part 3
Savouring the journey

11. The human engine: bicycling to Beijing

Chris Smith

Photo © Chris Smith

Chris Smith spent 13 months cycling 26,500 km (16,500 miles) from Worcestershire in the UK to Beijing in China. Since his return in 2001 he has clocked up a further 80,000 km (50,000 miles) by cycling to and from work. Smith's critically acclaimed book about his epic cycle trip from the UK to Beijing, *Why Don't You Fly?*, was shortlisted for the 2011 Rubery International Book Award. You can find more details at www.cycleuktochina.com Smith is currently working on his second book, *Karl Marx and Careful Driving*, an examination of what philosophy, history and the behaviour of fellow motorists tell us about the human condition.

I have long been a keen cyclist. Even before redundancy and the break-up of a long-term relationship gave me the opportunity to make the journey of a lifetime, I cycled from home to the office and back every day. 'Why don't you drive, Christopher?' my thunderstruck colleagues would ask.

Why didn't I drive? Like them, I could have driven to work in comfort with the heater turned up and the radio switched on. Instead I chose to cycle, no matter how cold, dark and wet it was, and I'd arrive at work on a high, having defeated the wind, rain and frost. The release of serotonin and endorphins are the body's way of thanking you for taking such good care of it, and the sense of general well-being you derive from being physically fit is beyond price. Cycling can also save you money; after all, there is no need to tax, insure, pay for official inspection of or put petrol into a bicycle.

'Aren't you frozen by the time you get home?'

Not at all: I arrive home radiating heat and energized by the exercise. Vigorous exercise thoroughly warms you from within. I never have starting problems in the winter and I don't have to scrape ice off the windscreen or struggle with frozen locks.

'Isn't that miles?'

Indeed it is! Twenty-five miles every day, 125 miles per week, and about 6,000 miles (9,700 km) a year. By providing a vigorous twice-daily workout, commuting by bicycle has made me extremely fit for a fraction of the cost of a gym membership.

I didn't drive to work for any number of excellent reasons, but above all because I have a perfectly good set of lungs and legs. The human body is a powerful, versatile and immensely sophisticated engine that thrives on hard work, but the power of the human engine continues to be underestimated by those who prefer to rely on the internal combustion engine, to the detriment of their health and the environment.

It is often said that even the longest journey begins with a single step, but I believe it begins well before that first step is taken. A journey begins with a dream or an idea. Unless you dream great dreams, it is unlikely that you will make a great journey. When I announced my intention to cycle halfway across the planet, a facetious friend said, 'Why don't you fly, Christopher? You'd be on the other side of the world within 18 hours instead of 18 months!'

There are two ways you can travel. Like my friend, you can journey to arrive as quickly as possible, in which case you buy your ticket, check in at Heathrow and board a jumbo jet. Within 12–15 hours you'll have arrived in Beijing or Bangkok, having crossed half the planet without seeing anything of it.

For 13 months I travelled independently. I was the master of my destiny, living on my wits and travelling exactly when, where and how I chose. Why don't you fly, Christopher? Because I intended to experience the fascinating variety of landscapes, climates, cultures and peoples that lie between Europe and the Far East.

I plotted a route through western, central and eastern Europe to Istanbul, and then through Turkey, Iran and Pakistan to India. It wasn't until I arrived in India that I decided to make Vladivostok my final destination in preference to Sydney or Perth. Unlike the route to Australia, the journey to the Russian Far East could be made entirely overland, via a return to Pakistan and a crossing of the Khunjerab Pass into China. I was intrigued by the physical challenge of following the spectacular Karakoram Highway over the 'stratospheric' 4,700 m (15,400 ft) Khunjerab Pass, and the prospect of tracing the legendary Silk Route through the remote areas of Chinese Turkestan.

There was no shortage of people questioning my sanity during the weeks and months leading up to departure. As I followed the Danube through central Europe, I started thinking that perhaps, after all, they had a point. I was having to adapt not only to cycling 130 km (80 mile) days, but also to life without a roof over my head, a comfortable bed, hot showers, central heating, the morning injection of caffeine, books, music at the press of a button, and so many of the other comforts that I had taken for granted.

I got up at sunrise and went to bed at dusk, sleeping rough to save money. I slept wherever it felt safe, which meant in places not frequented by other human beings. Woods were my first choice for shelter and concealment in Europe, but in the more arid landscapes of Iran, Baluchistan and Chinese Turkestan, I had to seek alternative shelter. Sometimes it would be a dried-up riverbed or one of the culverts running beneath the road, which provided shelter from wind or rain and were actually far more salubrious than some of the cockroach-infested budget hotels I stayed in.

For 13 months I never knew what each day would have in store or where I'd be laying out my sleeping bag at the end of it. It was a rough and gruelling way to travel, but it was remarkable how quickly I adapted both physically and psychologically to the task. My muscles hardened with the exercise, my skin became weathered by exposure to the elements, and my bones became accustomed to lying on hard and uneven surfaces. I got used to being alone and having no idea where I was going to wake up the following morning. Independent travel changes you externally and internally.

The joy of cycling, as opposed to travelling by bus, train, car or plane, is that you are exposed not only to a country's sights, but also to its sounds and smells, its sunshine, wind and rain, its dust, its insects and, of course, its people. As a Westerner on a bicycle I was a magnet for inquisitive locals all over Asia. People in the mountain villages of Turkey's Black Sea coast would ply me with glasses of tea and pepper me with questions whenever I stopped to buy food and drink. They spoke little English, but fortunately the Turks are nuts about European football, which has an international language of its own – one in which I happen to be fluent – so we got along very well.

I was apprehensive about my reception in Iran because of the anti-Western propaganda disseminated by the government, but most Iranians appear to take about as much notice of their politicians as we do of ours. They were friendly and hospitable in the roadside cafes and teahouses. If politicians and religious leaders would only emphasise our common humanity instead of exploiting ethnic and religious divides for their own ends, the world would surely be a much happier, safer and more prosperous place.

Bystanders in India and Pakistan emerged from apparently thin air and multiplied with extraordinary rapidity to lay siege to man and bicycle. Members of a 30-strong audience would rummage in my panniers, play with my tools, leaf through my diary and try on my sunglasses while I attempted to repair punctures at the roadside.

Restaurant owners in China would serve up delicious plates of food and, when they discovered where I was from and how I got there, they'd often refuse any payment. Sympathetic motorists would draw up alongside, usually while I was grinding my way up a steep hill, and the passenger would lean out to offer me a cigarette. It's the thought that counts. Most unexpected of all, even the Chinese police were friendly and cooperative.

Before I left home, people came up with some wonderfully romantic ideas about how I was going to die. I'd be shot by bandits, torn apart by wild animals or poisoned by snakes, and if by some miracle I escaped death, I'd be robbed and beaten up. Why don't you fly, Christopher?

You can choose to see the world either as generally safe with isolated pockets of danger or as generally dangerous with isolated pockets of safety. Living on £10 per day and my wits brought me respect, and even fascination.

Ordering food in China's roadside cafes and restaurants was usually met with blank incomprehension, and sometimes I would have to go into the kitchen and point to what I wanted, but the challenge of communication turned out to be part of the fun. I came to rely instinctively on actions, body language, facial expressions, gestures and tone of voice to convey meaning.

It was refreshing to encounter women in China after months travelling through countries in which they were either hidden away or it was taboo for them to approach strangers. I fell hopelessly and inappropriately in love with the wife of the proprietor in a roadside restaurant-cum-dormitory. We had not a word of language in common so we spent most of the evening smiling at each other. Whether or not she reciprocated my feelings is hard to say, but she was transparently fascinated by me. Although she was Chinese and I was English, these are superficial differences. We had our humanity in common. A smile is a sign of human solidarity that is understood the world over.

For 13 months my legs and lungs propelled my heavily loaded bicycle into headwinds and up to mountain passes. Like all engines, the body needs a ready supply of fuel. I was obliged to buy food and drink from supermarkets or petrol stations during the 3,800 km (2,400 mile) crossing of Europe. Beyond Istanbul the food became cheaper but it was also scarcer. You can't count on a McDonald's drive-through or an ice-cream van materialising in the middle of a desert just as you start to feel hungry, so I packed a titanium saucepan set and a multi-fuel stove, which could burn paraffin, petrol or diesel. This enabled me to purchase fuel from filling stations en route. My emergency rations consisted of packets of pasta and rice, because they are easy to cook, filling, lighter than tins and they don't go off. I carried water in three bottles mounted on the bicycle's frame. When crossing mountain areas or deserts where water was scarce, I stowed extra bottles of mineral water or fizz in my luggage. One discovery I made during this journey was that the most rudimentary dish of pasta and even a can of cold baked beans can be delicious if you're hungry enough – and when you are cycling between 130 and 160 km (80-100 miles) a day, you are almost constantly hungry.

I came to realize that brute strength and physical fitness, although indispensable, will only take you so far on a journey like this. As well as fuel, an engine needs a spark. For me, that spark was provided by passion. Passion drove me into headwinds and up to mountain passes when my feet were smarting, my crotch was sore and my back was aching. When I became ill in Pakistan and China and my strength and energy deserted me, passion was all that drove me on.

I think that everything people do should be motivated by passion. With sufficient passion you can overcome almost any obstacle – except perhaps bureaucracy. By denying me the visa that would have enabled me to cycle on to Vladivostok, the staff at the Russian embassy in Beijing finally succeeded where towering mountains, hurricane-force winds, scorching deserts, sandstorms, fever, food poisoning and saddle-soreness all failed. My journey ended prematurely at Tiananmen Square in Beijing.

My intention after getting to Vladivostok had been to take the Trans-Siberian express to Moscow and cycle home from there. I had imagined the final months of the journey so clearly. A final three-week push through Manchuria to the Russian border at Heihe was to have been followed by a two-week ride on rough roads from Blagoveshchensk to Vladivostok, where I'd have leaned the bicycle up in the city's central square to bask in my achievement. The six-day Trans-Siberian train ride across Russia to Moscow was to have been the ultimate reward for the previous months of toil: a glorious week of watching the Siberian landscape slide by without effort, aching or anxiety.

The power of that vision sustained me across two continents and 13 countries. I embarked on the ride to China not only to explore the world but also to discover my physical and mental limits. Much of the experience was tough and uncomfortable in the same way that running a marathon is tough and uncomfortable, but as in running a marathon (or in any activity that really extends you), overcoming the challenge is immensely satisfying: the greater the challenge, the greater the satisfaction. In choosing to cycle rather than fly, I actively sought adversity. The result was a thrilling voyage of external and internal discovery during which I experienced those rare moments of pure peace that only come with a sense of complete fulfilment.

Travelling to journey rather than to arrive involves a different attitude. Few people are able to abandon their commitments and responsibilities for sufficient time to cycle halfway across the world. However, flying to Biarritz or Benidorm to spend a fortnight in a hotel might be replaced by an alternative type of holiday – two weeks centred on a journey rather than a destination. Cycling is a great way to get to know a country and its people, and a planned cycling tour can provide an incentive to get fit. Flying has little to recommend it except speed. Travel by train or coach is a more comfortable way to experience a country.

Why don't you fly, Christopher? I didn't fly because I saw the journey as being more important (and so much more fascinating) than the destination. I think that can be taken as a parable for one's journey through life – the greatest journey of them all. During our journeys, wherever they may take us, there will be mountains to climb and the wind won't always be behind us. It is worth remembering, though, that it is not the freewheeling but these challenges that will make us stronger – and if it wasn't for the hills, there wouldn't be any freewheeling.

It's now the end of my journey. I have ridden my bicycle 26,500 km (16,500 miles) from my home in the UK to Beijing, a 13-month ride that has transformed me from Clark Kent into

Superman. During the ride from Worcestershire to Beijing I have worn out three sets of tyres, three chains, two sets of gears, two pairs of boots, and myself. The metamorphosis from Superman back to Clark Kent is achieved as soon as I check in the bike and panniers at Beijing airport.

From my seat next to the window I am able to watch as the ground drops away from beneath the Air China Boeing 747 during take-off. I can never help experiencing a faint feeling of misgiving at this point, for I have relinquished control of my destiny. Travelling by air is dependent travel. From now on my survival will depend on the skills of the pilot and co-pilot, the professionalism of the mechanics who last serviced the engines, and the ingenuity of the engineers who designed and built the aircraft.

Whereas in Asia I was subjected to a degree of scrutiny that in the West is the preserve only of celebrities, no one on this plane has any idea that I have just cycled across two continents. I have reverted from being extraordinary to ordinary.

Five hundred dollars of my money has purchased ten hours of polite indifference. I'm a package in a cargo, part of the plane's payload: collected in Beijing, sucked up into the air, and to be delivered to Frankfurt. Every activity around me in the plane is a routine, rehearsed thousands of times. It has to be. You can't afford the unexpected when you are 35,000 ft above the ground in a frail pressurized capsule. My neighbour tells me that we are flying over Russia. Thirty-five thousand feet below I can make out a flat, unpopulated landscape of forests and lakes and winding rivers glimmering silver in the sunshine: Siberia. Mesmerized by the sight unfolding below, I can feel only the most painful regret that I'm flying over one of the remotest places on earth, a mysterious land that has intrigued me since childhood. The faster you travel, the less you take in.

We land at Frankfurt airport at 6 p.m. local time after a 10-hour flight, crossing half the planet without seeing anything of it. I'm eager to collect my bike and bags as quickly as possible and cycle out of Frankfurt to find somewhere to sleep before it gets too late (and dark). We are herded like sheep into the immigration and baggage reclaim pens. The bike is at a separate counter for oversized baggage. I collect five of my bags from the carousel, but the sixth is a long time coming. When the belt jerks to a stop, the missing pannier is still not among the half-dozen remaining unclaimed suitcases. At the baggage tracing counter, they take the details and hand me a computer printout with a reference number and a phone number to ring. The pannier, one of the two smaller ones mounted on the front wheel, contains not only my expensive titanium saucepans, my stove, and all the tools and spares for the bike, but also my priceless, irreplaceable diaries.

At first I am overwhelmed by the disaster. I could have forgiven Air China the loss of any pannier other than that one. But as time has passed, the 13 months packed full of experience are still with me, and my passion for cycling – travelling through the world under my own steam, not over it at the mercy of others – has only been fuelled further.

12. Walking distance

Adam Weymouth

Photo © Sally Weymouth

Adam Weymouth is a writer and some-times walker. His work has appeared in various publications, including the *Guardian*, the *New Internationalist* and the *Ecologist*, and he has worked for a number of environmental organizations. He lives between Devon and Brittany, and he is currently writing a novel.

> Utopia is on the horizon: when I walk two steps, it takes two steps back ... I walk ten steps, and it is ten steps further away. What is utopia for? It is for this, for walking.
>
> (Eduardo Galeano, 1993, p. 211)

It took me 247 days to walk from England to Istanbul: 5,000 km (3,000 miles). Flight time is about 4 hours.

It certainly wasn't something I could have imagined doing a few years previously. There was a time when I flew a lot: America, Namibia, Australia and Namibia again. Those trips were impor-tant to me. Then, one summer break during university and at a loss for something to do, I walked for a month from the French/Spanish border to the cathedral city and pilgrim destination of Santiago de Compostela. It is an increasingly popular journey these days, and I met all sorts of people: devout Catholics, fitness fanatics, those looking for answers to a myriad of questions, and those looking for no more than a cheap and different sort of holiday. I wasn't doing it for religious reasons, or for environmental ones. But there was something meaningful about the walk that I couldn't quite put my finger on, and many of those that I spoke to said the same. I enjoyed myself immensely.

I flew back to England, retracing all those weeks of walking in a bit less than an hour. As I flew over mountains that I had crossed on foot, over those varying regions whose dialects I had come to know, I started to wonder what we might be losing when we travel at the speed of an aeroplane. Rather than seeing how the landscapes, the vegetation and the culture subtly shifted as I crossed the country step by step, I arrived back in London without seeing anything of the journey beyond the in-flight movie. But I kept on flying. I had too many places to see to bother with walking to all of them. Yet gradually, insidiously, my awareness of climate change was growing. I was reading more; it seemed to be forever in the news. On a climbing trip to Ecuador my guide pointed out how many hundreds of metres higher the snow line was than when he had seen it as a child. Flights were becoming more tinged with a guilt that the carbon offset websites seemed only temporarily to alleviate. I started to make changes in my own life: cycling, recycling, unplugging the phone charger. It felt inadequate in comparison to the scale of the problems I was reading about, or in comparison to the amount of snow that I hadn't seen in Ecuador. I started going on the annual climate-change march in London, carrying my placard, listening each year to the speakers in Grosvenor Square talking about all the things that needed to be done but weren't being done. Soon that didn't seem enough either.

So before long I found myself standing on the roof of the Scottish Parliament Building in Edinburgh as part of the anti-aviation group Plane Stupid. We were hanging a banner protesting against proposed runway expansions across Scotland. As the police and the television cameras stared up at us, I realized that flying was going to be difficult to justify to myself for much longer.

And so, about five years ago, I stopped flying altogether. It was an incredibly difficult decision to make. Having been lucky enough to travel a lot in the past certainly made the decision easier, but there were still so many places to visit, so many things that I wanted to do. The prospect of a lifetime of damp holidays spent on English beaches seemed bleak. I started wondering whether it would be possible to have comparable adventures which did not involve going to such far-flung parts of the globe. And I began to think once again about walking. It took a couple of years of planning, but finally, in the early spring of 2010, with the trees still bare and the fields freshly ploughed, I left the village of Whiteparish, near Salisbury, and followed the paths through the forests towards London, taking the first steps on a journey whose beauty and challenges I could never have imagined.

A fortnight later, in Canterbury, I was ushered into the cathedral through the pilgrims' entrance. I stood on the worn stones at Becket's tomb, where countless wanderers had stood before me, and thought about the journey that stretched ahead. Two days later I was in Dover. Across the Channel lay France, and beyond that – far, far beyond that, I was beginning to realize – lay Turkey. The next morning I boarded the ferry, and left the white cliffs behind for the next seven and a half months.

I began with an idea that walking, more than any other form of transport, forces you to engage with everyone and everything that you pass. Yet I quickly found that this is not always a pleasant experience. Studying maps at home before setting out, I had not planned for the days of endless boredom, trudging through landscapes so humanised that they are no longer human-sized. In the north of France I walked through village after village that had long since had its community ripped out by the advance of second homes, commuters and agribusiness, the cafes and schools now closed. The fields between them were enormous and the trees cut down, and I could hardly stand in the winds. Far in the distance I aimed for the next squat grey church, head bent against a storm.

And then came Paris. It took me two days to reach the centre of the city from the beginnings of its suburbs. I spent the first night in Charles de Gaulle airport, and then walked through the endless sprawl of business parks, car showrooms and shanty towns propped up by motorway flyovers. It was interesting, but profoundly depressing: places we can only see comfortably through the eyes of a machine, moving at a machine's speed. I began to wonder if it is the very fact that we are able to forget about these places, zipping through them or flying over them, that allows us to desecrate them guilt-free and to ignore the people who are forced to live there. Perhaps if we had to engage with these places we would take more care of them. Walking seems one way of trying to recognize all parts of this world, in its sickness and its health.

Yet walking is in a fast and remarkable decline. A study by the Department of Transport in the UK found that between 1995 and 2010 the average number of journeys by foot per person fell by 28 per cent, from 292 to 210 annually, and that 20 per cent of people walked a 20-minute journey less than once a year (Department of Transport, 2011). 'Walking distance' is considered by town planners to be roughly a quarter of a mile (DeRubertis, 2008). These figures are astounding, yet such a change is not a new phenomenon. As long ago as 1862, in his essay 'Walking' Henry David Thoreau bemoaned that we had come to live 'as if legs were made for sitting on, not walking' (2004, p. 3).

The eighteenth century saw the rise of a new type of tourism – tourism of the 'picturesque'. The word first appeared in the *Oxford*

English Dictionary of 1703 with the definition 'in the manner of a picture; fit to be made into a picture'. A picturesque traveller was described by art historian Christopher Hussey as one who had 'a conception of an ideal form of nature, derived from landscape painting' (cited in Hooper, 2002, p. 174). William Gilpin, artist, cleric and one of the best-known writers on the subject, suggested in a work of 1782 that we examine 'the face of a country *by the rules of picturesque beauty*', and in a later book went on to say that his writing was intended to '*characterize the countries* through which the reader is carried' (cited in Hooper, 2002, p. 175 (italics original)). This new breed of tourist made their way through landscapes in their horse-drawn coaches, paint box or pen in hand, taking the world's first holiday snaps.

It was at this time that 'the business of travel began to be distinguished from the activity of walking' (Ingold, 2004, p. 321). The affluent began to see walking as something beneath them, a form of travelling that was literally a travail, even though the carriage was neither much faster nor a much more comfortable alternative. It is an idea that 'lingers in the residual connotations of the word "pedestrian" ' (p. 321). If walking did have to be endured it received barely a mention in the traveller's accounts. Years later we have in-flight films, DVDs in cars and cries from the back seat of 'Are we there yet?' Such disregard for the journey is impossible as a pedestrian.

Certainly, as a means of getting from A to B, walking does not make much sense. It's tiring, the hills are exhausting, the blisters are awful and you can't take much with you. Sponsored walks recognize this. If people are going to put themselves through walking 30 km (20 miles), don't they at least deserve some money? But despite its impracticalities, I began to see that walking also has its benefits – benefits that come when we stop thinking about where we are going and instead enjoy where we are on the journey.

From Paris I traced the Seine to Dijon as spring finally came to France. After a month on the flat, the hills began to rise before me in slowly growing folds. I followed the pine forests of the Vosges down to Geneva, and then began to climb in earnest until I was surrounded by the vastness of the Swiss-French Alps, the snow still thick on the ground in May. I spent several weeks making my way through them, climbing over almost impenetrable passes watched by chamois, drinking from the snow melt, sitting alone in small refuges in the evening with the wood burner lit and my dinner simmering on top. Finally, at 2,477 m (8,127 ft), at the Col de Clapier, the border still threaded with rusting barbed wire from other times, I emerged into Italy and into the summer. As I descended the slopes into the valley of Susa, yellow acacia trembled in the wind and I stopped to pick the first wild strawberries of the year.

From Turin I made my way south to Genoa and followed the cliffs of the Ligurian coast for several days, swimming every morning and evening, fuelling myself on the local focaccia and pesto. The temperature rose into the 40s and Italy limped out of the World Cup, closely followed by England. I crossed the country along the spine of the Apennines – smaller, more crowded mountains than the Alps, receding in misty layers into the south. In bars at night I was served local cheeses as people muttered about the corruption of their government. Back on the plains I walked the delta of the Po as it widened towards the sea, and eventually came to the beginning of the Balkans.

On the border with Croatia the customs official sat me down in his office and we toasted my arrival to his country with rakija, the ubiquitous local spirit. I felt a very long way from England. Yet despite vast differences in culture, from England to Turkey I was looked after by the generosity of strangers to an extent that I could never have imagined before I set out. I was invited into people's houses for coffee, for a Sunday lunch, for a bed. I was allowed to sleep in barns, in churches and in mosques. I spent evenings in bars to find at the end that some unknown person had paid for me. I was given oranges and Easter eggs, and shared meals in restaurants and at mountain passes. And I was shown friendship at times when I really needed it.

Just as we assume that those huge fields and suburbs do not exist in our world, we are prone to assume that hospitality no longer exists either. Two years ago a friend of mine walked from Edinburgh to London, barefoot and without money, among other things as an exploration of hospitality in the twenty-first century. A bishop advised him that he should ask for nothing except water. To ask, he said, would be to rob people of the opportunity of offering. It seems that many constructs of our world – flights, fear of strangers, obsessions about safety and security – are robbing people of the same chance.

In the Bible, the word often translated as 'hospitality' is the Greek *philoxenia*, a love of strangers. And this goes both ways, for in a hospitable relationship each is a stranger to the other – it is about recognizing both the other within oneself and oneself in the other. The exchange feels reciprocal in a way that is hard to pin down. We share a conversation, a friendship, the age-old human act of two people connecting over a gift. Furthermore, it does not feel like a one-off exchange, but more like the continuation or recommencement of a circle of hospitality which increasingly needs to be refreshed to be maintained. Yet the opportunities to connect with strangers are few, and they are decreasing. Walking through people's villages I felt like a rare beast, and found people almost eager to invite me into their houses, to share stories. I know of no better way than a walk to remind us of the importance of openness to strangers.

I descended into former Yugoslavia, walking through dusty limestone mountains that I was told still hid wolves and bears, skirting the edges of minefields, following the turquoise seas of the Croatian coast. Old Ottoman influences started to entwine with the Catholic, and my days were punctuated with the call to prayer drifting across the landscapes. Everyone had stories to tell about the war, knew someone affected by it or had fought in it themselves. Walls were still riddled with bullet holes, and different ethnic groups bristled side by side. Each border was heavy with distrust, and each new country welcomed me ever more openly.

Maps became harder to come by but it mattered less. With very little private land and barely any fences, I could simply point my compass south-east and walk, getting directions from the shepherds. I followed old pathways and donkey trails, routes through the mountains that had been worn by the drovers, armies and wanderers before me, lines that spoke of human habit and an intimate connection with the world. Walking has always tied people to the land, and we have sculpted that land, but with the gentleness of human feet rather than the rapaciousness of human hands.

The summer was fading, the nights longer, and I was eating walnuts and apples from the trees and finding mushrooms in the forests. One morning in Bulgaria I woke with ice on the inside of my tent and footprints of wolves in the first snows outside. I rushed through the last mountains of eastern Europe as the autumn mists drew in across the pines.

Everyone walks, and I think this is one reason why people appreciated the story that I was carrying. Whether one walks to the shops or to Istanbul, the process is the same – it simply comes down to the number of footsteps you take before you stop. Walking was, I came to see, a fairly mundane thing to do, and because of that it was something that people could relate to. I wasn't telling a dramatic story of distant travel and fast experiences. I was simply putting one foot in front of the other, just the same as them.

In her wonderful book *Wanderlust* (2000), Rebecca Solnit sug-gests that the mind works at 3 miles per hour (5 km/hr). We have evolved to engage with our land at this pace, and anything faster is in some ways a reduction. People are unique among animals in performing almost all their travelling sitting down. Whether on a bike, or in a bus or car, we glide across the surface of our world. Our mind can be entirely elsewhere as we travel from A to B, disconnected from the places through which it passes, asleep at the wheel. To walk returns and retunes us to the natural rhythms of our bodies. Walking's restorative powers are well recognized in all religions of the world, and that is one reason for the pervasiveness of pilgrimage. In a world that moves faster than ever before, the simple act of walking is increasingly radical, necessary and sane.

The *Beyond Belief* report by the World Wildlife Fund and the Alliance of Religions and Conservation (2006) looks at the importance of faith in protecting sacred sites. The report chooses two paths as case studies: the song lines in Australia and the pil-grimage to Santiago de Compostela in Spain. In relation to San-tiago de Compostela, the authors write:

> The Way provides a closer relationship with outstanding protected natural areas, significant sacred sites, and centres of spiritual and cultural heritage, as well as close contacts with people from all strands of life, which usually produces, or reinforces, a more conscious and respectful attitude towards the universal values of our common heritage.
> (p. 108)

Walking gives us time to develop these connections in a way that faster means of transport do not. It is a speed that the earth is comfortable with. Our legs are the hands of the clock of the earth.

The nineteenth century *flâneur* of Baudelaire's Paris attempted to remove his walking (for it was invariably a 'he') from the mechanical rhythms that beat time in the modern city. *Flânerie* (literally translated from the French as 'sauntering', but embodying a more comprehensive philosophy) was a quiet rebellion against the two driving capitalist imperatives of the city – to be in a hurry and to shop (Botton, 1999). *Flâneurs* were, in Baudelaire's phrase, 'botanist[s] of the sidewalk' (Smart and Tester, 1994, p.160), strolling the boulevards for hours and observing all they saw: a lovers' spat, a passing glance from a half-seen stranger, a store window studied not for shopping but to better understand shoppers, the loud and the lonely and all the lives of the city. Some took tortoises on leads to set the pace. Through being aware of all that was around him, Baudelaire believed he could develop a new sort of community in the city and ultimately come to feel at home everywhere.

I'm not advocating a return to a cosseted and dandyish Parisian lifestyle that many would see as downright pretentious, but there are ideas here worth exploring. Flights are the very opposite of *flânerie*. The word 'utopia' derives from the Greek *ou*, 'not', and *topos*, 'place'. It is literally 'no place', a place that does not exist. Short of teleportation, flying is about as utopian as our travelling is likely to get. Ignoring any sense of place between the two airports, we arrive comparatively instantaneously with none of the exertion that is required to make the journey overland – but, like all utopias, this one is an illusion. The energy required to make the journey is merely displaced to where we cannot see it. We may not leave any footprints in the earth, but we leave heavy carbon footprints above it.

I realize that not everyone can set out tomorrow on a year-long walk. I have told my story merely to kindle ideas of what might be possible, of how travel today might differ from its previous incarnations and how our planet, and we ourselves, might suffer as a result. What if systems were in place to allow everybody to take a long walk at some time in their life? It is not entirely fanciful. The Camino de Santiago has a system of cheap and free accommodation that allows pilgrims to walk according to their means, and the number of walkers is increasing exponentially, from 7,000 in 1991 to 118,000 in 2001, to 183,000 in 2011 (American Pilgrims on the Camino, 2011). Since the 1980s, the Flemish organization Oikoten has been offering young offenders the chance to walk to Santiago de Compostela from Belgium, with a mentor, as an alternative to being locked in an institution, and it has had a remarkable degree of success (Weymouth, 2012).

My aim is to suggest that travel has more functions than simply finding what you set out to experience. Maybe we need to restore an element of travail to travel, forcing us to engage with the whole of our world in whatever ways it presents itself, and to acknowledge both the generosity of strangers and the unloved, uncared-for parts of our world that are often just a few miles from where we live.

Eight months after I had started, I came to Istanbul. I had crossed Europe, at a speed unchanged since humans took their first tottering steps on two legs out of the forests. I came to the Golden Horn long after night had fallen and sat down, my feet raw. After months of imagining this moment, I felt a little underwhelmed. Further along the bank a small group of fishermen were coming to the end of their dinner. They called me over and offered me grapes and rakija, and I explained with my handful of Turkish words what I was up to.

Despite the wonderful hospitality I had received throughout my journey, I had assumed I would never find it in a city of 13 million people – especially when it seemed like every other person had a rucksack on their back. But as we finished eating they told me proudly that the only way to see their city was from the water, and invited me out in their boat.

The skipper clamped a cigarette in his teeth and warned me that once we were out in the bay there would be a lot of waves, so we'd have to keep moving fast and hold on. We passed beneath the bridges of the Golden Horn and into the mouth of the Bosphorus, and there was Asia, the mile-long bridge threading the continents together, the mosques and the palaces, all the millions of lights on the water and us bouncing in a tiny boat across the waves, darting among the ferries and the cargo ships. I had walked from England to the beginnings of Asia, and here I was going to stop. From across the bay blew warm winds that spoke of other continents, and I felt as though, finally, I had arrived.

References

American Pilgrims on the Camino (2011). 'Compostelas issued by the Oficina de Acogida de Peregrinos by year'.
Retrieved from www.americanpilgrims.com/camino/statistics.html

Botton, A. de. A good idea from... Baudelaire. *Independent*, 9 May 1999. Retrieved from www.independent.co.uk/arts-entertainment/alain-de-botton-column-1092588.html

Department of Transport (2011). *National Travel Survey 2010.* Retrieved from www.dft.gov.uk/statistics/releases/national-travel-survey-2010/

DeRubertis, D. (2008). 'Is "walking distance" overrated?' Retrieved from www.planetizen.com/node/31270

Galeano, E. (1993). *Las Palabras Andantes*. Montevideo: Siglo XXI Ediciones.

Hooper, G. (2002). 'The Isles/Ireland: The wilder shore'. In P. Hulme and T. Young (eds.), *The Cambridge Companion to Travel Writing*. Cambridge University Press.

Ingold, T. (2004). 'Culture of the ground: The world perceived through the feet'. *Journal of Material Culture*, 9(3): 315–40.

Smart, B. and Tester, K. (1994). *The Flâneur*. New York: Routledge.

Solnit, R. (2000). *Wanderlust*. New York: Viking.

Thoreau, H. D. ([1862] 2004). *Walking*. Whitefish: Kessinger Publishing.

Weymouth, A. (2012). 'Redemption road'. *New Internationalist*, No 454: 20–2. Retrieved from www.newint.org/features/2012/07/01/redemption-road-pilgrimage/

World Wildlife Fund and Alliance of Religions and Conservation (2006). *Beyond belief: Linking faiths and protected areas to support biodiversity conservation*. Retrieved from www.arcworld.org/downloads/WWF%20Beyond%20Belief.pdf

13. bike2oz: the world going through you instead of around you

Lowanna Doye
(with assistance from Beth Edwards and Jonathan King)

Photo © Lowanna Doye

Lowanna Doye's environmentalism began in her teens when she co-founded an eco club for students at her high school. A visual arts degree at Australia's Newcastle University saw her major in photography and video. Post-university her dual passions were unified in her work for Undercurrents, an Oxford-based environmental and social justice video-zine. When she met fellow video activist Kev Doye, the bike2oz dream was born. They now live with their four children in an off-the-grid eco house in Bellingen, on the east coast of Australia, where they run a thriving organic grocery store focused on supporting local growers.

It was 1997 and I was in my mid-20s, working as a volunteer in Oxford at the alternative news videozine Undercurrents, assisting the small team to compile honest video reports about local and global social justice and environmental issues. I was working late into the night, assisting the editor to cut a film explaining global warming, when the concept for the bike2oz expedition first dawned on me.

Splicing various soundtracks for the piece, I listened over and over to the narrator's voice claiming that air travel was the single biggest contributor to global warming – the single biggest! As we previewed reels of footage, an idea came to me. A passionate environmentalist, I had developed a belief that every individual has the potential to contribute to the environmental movement. I had to live by my principles, I thought. So, in the wee hours of that autumn morning, I contemplated my own situation: I was an Australian backpacker who had been affluent enough to fly to Europe for my post-university travel experience. But now, further politicised by my reports for Undercurrents, I decided on the spot that I would cycle home to Australia rather than contribute to global warming by booking yet another airline ticket. After making this spontaneous decision, I felt relieved. Now I had a plan with a purpose.

At first I was determined to cycle alone, inspired by the likes of travel writers Dervla Murphy, Anne Mustoe and Josie Dew. But it wasn't until I shared my idea with my partner at the time, fellow film-making environmentalist Kev Doye, that the idea really started to take shape. The cycle journey became an environmental expedition to raise awareness of global warming. We would use our collective skills in journalism, photography and film-making to document this massive undertaking, and interview climate-change campaigners en route. bike2oz was born.

Preparation

We began to prepare, and although I had originally dreamed of riding solo like the other intrepid female cyclists, I soon realized we would make a great combination. I had an abundance of ideas and optimism, whereas Kev was brilliantly practical. Within a day or so of deciding to cycle with me, he dragged me down to Brighton's library, where we pulled out big old atlases and weather books. We tried to design the most direct and least mountainous route. Kev began to study the weather patterns en route, trying to predict the optimum time of year to be pedalling through each country. Once the expedition was under way, there were many occasions when Kev's passion for and expertize in meteorology saved us from minor disaster. His practicality, enthusiasm and focus transformed the dream into a reality, and enabled us to create a timeline and lock in a departure date.

Before the expedition we owned second-hand mountain bikes, so we were amazed to find how effortless cycling became when we swapped the old '3-speeds' for something designed for comfort. Fortunately, we befriended a visionary at the UK Dawes Cycles headquarters, who agreed to our dream suggestion: in exchange for two of their famous touring bikes – their renowned Super Galaxy models – we would promote their product as the ideal bike for challenging expeditions.

Sight-seeing vehicles travel incredibly fast, and the windows of cars, trains and tourist coaches create a separation between people and the places they are travelling through. On our bicycles we would experience first-hand every smell and temperature extreme, and while this immersion in the local culture would make us vulnerable, the intensity of this interaction would provide a deeper, richer travel experience and would become a catalyst for profound personal change. Kev summed it up one day in the saddle with the words: 'the world going through you instead of around you'.

The expedition begins

After months of anticipation the big day finally came. On a chilly winter's morning – 1 February 2000 – we wobbled away from home near Oxford on our bicycles. Praying we had not forgotten anything, we felt the enormous weight of our panniers that were packed to the brim. A heavy video camera was bungeed to the handlebars recording this long-awaited moment of departure – plus we carried its trusty tripod and a laptop in Kev's back pannier. (A custom-made solar panel would be sent to us en route when we reached Italian sunshine.) I thought of Dervla Murphy, decades earlier, tearing pages out of her paperback novels once she had read them, to lighten the load in her panniers!

Almost skidding on the icy road in the early dawn, we felt scared and excited at the same time. We planned to pedal across 16 countries over the next 15 months to prove that you can cross the world without flying. We hoped we were prepared for what lay ahead.

Our promise never to fly was tested early in the journey. While cycling painfully slowly into a cold headwind through the Netherlands, we pedalled right past luxury airliners at Schiphol airport. The reality of our undertaking hit home: we could simply throw our bikes and panniers on one of those Boeing 737s and be in sunny Sydney in a staggeringly fast 24 hours. Instead we were choosing to pedal overland to Australia – a journey that would take nearly twice as long as my ancestor Lt Philip Gidley King's journey to Sydney in 1788 in his square-rigged sailing ship.

We turned away from the temptation of the aeroplanes, put our heads down and rode on into the wind. But from that moment onwards we developed a coping mechanism that stayed with us for the rest of the expedition. In order to deal with the distance that seemed to stretch out before us, we needed to cast Sydney – our final port of call – out of our minds. We decided to take one day at a time, simply riding as far as we could, free-camping where possible and celebrating each manageable milestone. This was one of the many strategies we developed that got us home.

Across Europe and Asia

After Schiphol airport we began to experience a sense of time-lessness on the journey, as though we had entered a different dimension. From then on we didn't compare cycling with driving or flying: it just became what we did. Nevertheless, within hours of crossing on to the overcrowded roads of Belgium, I had my first accident, which again tested my resolve. Although unhurt, I was frozen by the cold, shaken by the accident and had my first meltdown – which Kev filmed – complaining that I did not want to carry that 'bloody camera' all the way to Australia. The physical strain of lugging the film-making gear, not to mention the emotional strain of feeling the pressure to record almost every experience we were encountering, had begun to take its toll. In the cold conditions of a north European winter we came very close to ditching the film idea entirely, and almost posted the equipment back to the UK.

Our commitment to our environmental expedition was strength-ened when we reached France and cycled through forests devastated by recent storms, dodging kilometres of beautiful trees lying on their sides. I filmed my own private weatherman, Kev, describing this traumatized landscape and suggesting that such storms could become more frequent if carbon emissions continued to increase.

By holding onto that camera we were able to interview cycle experts in most countries en route and, by sending the film cas-settes to a morning television programme in Australia, we hoped that our message would reach a wider audience and inspire others to make greener choices – such as leaving the car at home and cycling to work. This purpose certainly helped justify carrying the equipment over the Alps in Switzerland – an environmentally cleaner country, with a national network of cycleways, which, as an illustration of what was possible, galvanized our commitment to continue to Sydney without flying.

Crowded Italy challenged us further, because the crazy drivers seemed to take no notice of our bikes at all, a perception confirmed by a local cycling campaigner we filmed who reported that there were few bike lanes and on average one cyclist a week was killed. By chance we rode into Genoa on 'Car-free Day', when people took to the streets to enjoy peaceful, traffic-free open space, complete with entertainment and a carnival atmosphere. It seemed at least one local council was aware of the problem. And there was no shortage of bikes either, as we saw when the Giro D'Italia cycle race just happened to whizz past us during one lunch stop.

Although Switzerland and Italy had their share of hills, we were surprised to find that the mountain passes in Greece were on another scale altogether. A local campaigner who ran a cycle shop in one of the traffic-choked towns told us on film that we – or at least I – would not get through. 'Why not?' I asked. 'Because you are not a man!' was his matter-of-fact reply. Although his comment quietly enraged me, it gave me all the rocket fuel I needed to pedal over that mountain pass.

Greece marked another expedition turning-point for us. As we reached the peak of a particularly intense climb, I had a flash: that it was the psychological rather than the physical barrier that we had broken through. We had conquered our fear of climbing. In the same way that we had earlier shifted our focus to 'one day at a time', in Greece we developed a 'one pedal at a time' meditation for getting us up the mountains in the scorching dry heat. It felt like a milestone as we bade farewell to Europe, crossing the Aegean Sea by ferry and entering Turkey. Australians had first fought here in the First World War, so we left our heavy panniers at the youth hostel and pedalled on a pilgrimage to pay our respects to the Diggers – many younger than me – who had died at Gallipoli in 1915.

That was the quiet before the storm. As we left Istanbul, everything was on a bigger scale: large skies, long straight roads heading east, deadly potholes and enormous trucks hogging the road and hurtling towards us. Perhaps even more than in Italy, we felt the need for protection on the Turkish roads. Having consciously chosen not to wear cycle helmets (based on UK studies that claimed cyclists were, surprisingly, safer without) we emailed my parents in Sydney, who posted two helmets out to us. We pedalled east through the Turkish 'outback', passing Mount Ararat, where the Ark is supposed to have sheltered after Noah used it to survive what was possibly an environmental catastrophe thousands of years ago – a massive sea-level rise known then as the 'Great Flood'.

There was very little water, however, once we got to the Iranian city of Esfahan. I filmed Kev walking past marooned paddle boats on the dry riverbed of the wide Zayandeh River, suggesting to camera that the devastating drought Iran was experiencing, including a cholera outbreak and massive livestock loss, was quite possibly connected to global warming.

Cycling over the border into India I spotted a woman ahead on a bicycle. Pedalling gracefully, she was dressed in a floral sari with her long hair pulled back into a plait. Overcome with emotion, I shed tears of solidarity, because I had not seen another woman cycling since the northern cities of Italy. Traversing southern Italy, Greece, Iran and Pakistan, I had at times felt like a freak, constantly attracting attention from onlookers and other road users. On one particular stretch of road in Pakistan, I had counted more than a hundred offensive comments (before lunchtime!) shouted at us from the roadside, most of them sexual in their content. On days like those I felt relief that I had not embarked on this journey alone, as had been my initial intention. As we cycled towards Amritsar I felt the comforting promise of a little more anonymity in this land.

But although it was a relief to blend into the surroundings, India challenged us environmentally and physically. We filmed a transport expert at a university in Delhi describing her ambitious vision for a cycle-friendly sustainable transport plan for the city. However, back on our bikes in the crazy traffic we despaired of this big city, easily one of the most polluted we had seen on our expedition. The streets were choked with stationary vehicles, the majority of which were little yellow taxis blowing their horns and belching out fumes. The sky was brown and the air gritty. After a few nights in the capital we had developed flu-like symptoms, with aching muscles and sore throats, which disappeared as soon as we pedalled out of the city. It could have been a virus, but at the time we were convinced it was a symptom of the pollution. These moments, though testing, also reignited our commitment to travel sustainably to Australia.

At the time of departure our research had led us to believe that air travel consumed 37 times more energy than sea travel, so with that in mind we secured a passage on a cargo ship from Mumbai to Singapore.

Compared with India, the atmosphere in Singapore was clean, and the traffic (mostly crowded buses) free-flowing, with spacious lanes for bikes and pedestrians, and plenty of flourishing tree-filled parks acting as carbon sinks. We had finally found a city where town planners had taken significant environmental steps. As this was the last foreign city on our overland expedition, we were encouraged.

The home stretch

It took a four-week search to locate a cargo ship that agreed to transport us with our bikes to Australia. After eight refreshing days at sea we landed safely in Brisbane and began to ride south on an inland route towards our destination: Sydney. Cycling along clean, open roads, under clear blue skies, Kev fell in love with the landscapes of my childhood.

The pace quickened as we headed south from my old university town of Newcastle, and the roads filled with cars as we approached Sydney. Nevertheless, on 3 May 2001 we rode proudly across the Sydney Harbour Bridge, around Circular Quay and the corner beside Farm Cove, where in front of us – adding to our excitement as we approached Mrs Macquarie's Chair – stretched the yellow finish-line tape, the welcoming committee, and a media contingent waiting to take our photos and hear our story. As champagne corks popped, I cast my mind back to Schiphol airport in the Netherlands, with its bitter winds and tempting aeroplanes. We had come a long way.

Travelling slowly across the surface of the Earth we had learned more about the cultures and religions en route than we might have done, had we travelled using faster modes of transport. We had connected more deeply to places and earned respect (and incredulity!) from people who knew we could afford to fly and had chosen to cycle instead.

Although we both had our fair share of sickness, for the majority of the expedition we had enjoyed the feeling of extreme physical fitness that comes with that level of exercise. Each time we passed across a nation's border we were filled with a huge sense of satisfaction, knowing that we had crossed that great mass of land using our own fuel to power our vehicles.

Even though more than a decade has passed since we completed our expedition, we continue to observe that our journey inspires others to choose more challenging yet also more rewarding transport options. As I work on the final draft of this chapter, I am in conversation with a Canadian cycle tourist who tracked us down through the internet to ask our advice about cycling through Asia, and an Australian couple seeking last-minute tips for their long-distance international cycle journey. It is an honour to help because I am deeply passionate about the multiple benefits of cycling.

After 485 days, 16 countries and 12,000 km (7,500 mile) of pedalling, we had achieved our goal of travelling only by sustainable transport from England to Australia, saving vast quantities of greenhouse gas emissions, and actively challenging the preconception that flying is the only option for travelling long distances.

14. A small matter of distance: trying not to fly to climate talks

Nic Seton

Photo © Sarah Golden

Nic Seton is a child of the eighties. Born in Australia, he grew up with mobile phones, the internet and the UN Framework Convention on Climate Change. His interest in local environmental events led to a degree in environmental studies, and student life led to activism. As part of the Australian Youth Climate Coalition he travelled, by train and bus, to the 2008 UN Climate Change Conference in Poznan, Poland. After the conference, he migrated to the UK and has been campaigning on climate change ever since. He is now a digital campaigner at Greenpeace.

I left Brisbane on a Greyhound bus in late September 2008. It took three days to get to Darwin, three days in which I saw more of Australia than in the rest of my lifetime. Through forests of ant hills, some three metres tall, past mining towns, truck stops, and one cyclist who braved the long hot highways alone. I began to develop a mental picture of my home and roots, something to take with me.

I didn't know when I'd be back, and I didn't know that I was saying goodbye to some of my family for ever. But through my studies, I had come to understand that climate change is real and, in a classically youthful approach, I was eager to make a difference. So I chose to embark on a journey to the 2008 UN Climate Change Conference in Poznan, Poland. I chose to travel in a way that avoided a significant impact on the climate; that meant not flying. Instead, my companions and I planned a journey overland from Australia, avoiding the Himalayas, traversing east and north Asia to arrive in late November. Previously, I'd always thought the only distance between me and my ancestral past in Europe was an economy-class flight. Now I would find out: after all, how hard could it be to travel without flying?

I met two of my companions – Ollie from Sydney and Anna from Brisbane – at the Darwin bus station. Our first leg across Australia had been a success. That week we canvassed the town trying to find a way across the surface of the Timor Sea to Indonesia. But storm season was approaching, sailing masts were coming down, and working boats wouldn't compromise on corporate policies that deny passenger fares. We were losing time and the people we asked didn't understand why we wouldn't want to fly. After unsuccessful phone calls, leafleting and radio interviews explaining our mission, we gave in and opted for the shortest possible connection on our route: Darwin to Singapore. This would be our one and only flight; the only leg where there was no other option.

We tried not to let a 3,300 km (2,050 mile) flight dampen our resolve. After all, we had each travelled more than that without flying, and we still had 16,442 km (10,216 mile) to go.

I have been involved in climate activism for ten years and the matter of emissions associated with flying has been a constant concern. Flying to get to a climate conference? I wanted to see what it was like to get there with the smallest dump of fresh greenhouse gases into a greenhouse that really doesn't need them.

The realization, militarisation and commercialisation of aviation gave birth to the institution of human flight. Aviation has grown year on year; as incomes increased, more people could afford to fly. What's more, in countries like the UK, aviation has received generous subsidies, from tax-free fuel to infrastructure. Social and environmental costs are generally ignored. Sadly, aviation is symbolic of the inequality of globalisation: people with higher incomes fly much more than those on lower incomes (Committee on Climate Change, 2009), while those on lower incomes disproportionately shoulder the consequences.

Flight has long occupied people's dreams and stories. According to Greek mythology, Icarus dreamed of flying and thought he'd succeeded – until he flew too high and the sun melted his wax wings. Now human flight is taking its toll. The unmitigated growth in aviation emissions will exacerbate climate change. Our power to fly requires a collective responsibility to manage the use of jet aircraft. Governments have yet to act on this responsibility, and a minority of conscientious consumers will not be enough to effect change. Action must come from both a concerned citizenship and a responsible regulation – a fact that is becoming increasingly difficult to hide. In that light, you could see our journey as a small act of collective responsibility.

So on 1 October, Anna, Ollie and I waited to meet our friends Katy and Jack at the arrivals gate at Singapore's giant Changi airport. Aged between sixteen and twenty-six, the five of us were to travel together from that point overland to the UN Climate Change Conference. Five hundred young people from over fifty countries were to attend the conference that year, not as representatives of governments or NGOs, but as concerned young people representing themselves. We did not want to be left out of the discussions for fear that they would fail to live up to the basic recommendations of conservative climate scientists. And we did not want to leave the process to politicians and traditional media, for fear they would tout slow progress as effective diplomacy and justify a lack of coverage by perceived demand.

In Singapore we met other young people who, like us, shared a vision for a world without social and environmental problems. Many of them we would see again as youth delegates in Poland. We enjoyed their hospitality and their city for three days. Coinciding with our visit, the government put on its greenest public-relations exercise with the opening of a marina barrage: a 10,000-hectare freshwater security catchment in the heart of a growing island city that imports its water. Our Singaporean hosts were at the event to promote their youth initiative, ECO Singapore, which supports green lifestyles.

With new friendships and the promise of reunion, we boarded our first train, destination Penang, Malaysia. The train was old but comfortable, with rows of curtained beds along the carriage sides. At night, we listened to the tracks beneath our pillows as the train clambered through the jungle and rocked us to sleep.

Travelling by routes that are ignored by airlines, I was struck by the difference in travel experiences. The old station in Singapore was decorated with twentieth-century posters advertising golden train trips along the Malaysian, Thai and Vietnamese coastlines. Our journey did not disappoint, with endless scenes of natural and cultural significance right outside the window. Time is a small price to pay for the humanity, spirituality and personal reflections that come with a long-distance journey on ancient routes.

Shortly before arrival in Penang, we awoke to a sea of oil palm, a monocrop that finds its way into an array of consumer items and aviation fuels. Throughout Malaysia and Thailand we saw forests being cleared and replanted with rubber trees and more oil palm, damaging the ecosystem, impacting water cycles, and hindering the areas' natural disaster protection. Plantations that require the destruction of natural forest also diminish the area's ability to absorb and store carbon, while releasing vast amounts of previously secure greenhouse gases. In broken English we conversed with fellow passengers who shared our food and relayed the history of the region to us. What had been virgin forest during our lifetime had become the scene of global industry.

After two days' travelling, we rested for two days in busy Bangkok, where we met other young climate activists. We explored the parks and markets and witnessed spontaneous political demonstrations over the disputed corruption of the then Thaksin government.

Our next train left us in Aranyaprathet, which was as far as trains would travel towards Cambodia. The ticket cost less than a Marsbar, and we were lucky to get seats. In a crowded carriage we led an impromptu singalong with fellow travellers to pass the time. Near the Thai border, the sun was strong and the roads were entirely made of dust. After acquiring our visa from an isolated and informal office near Poipet, we crossed the international border, through grandiose gates that spoke of pride in the once-powerful Khmer empire.

The west Cambodian transport network was made up of pot-holed and flooded roads, and was dominated by a clever cartel of vehicle operators who were happy to watch us ask around for competition. Naturally we paid the price for being tourists. A private bus took us to Sisophon and a private taxi drove all five of us down to Battambang, where we spent the night in an old colonial hotel. Before bed, we went looking for some local cuisine and spent the evening eating crickets and frogs with a generous group of local taxi drivers who were partial to black rice wine. It was a Lonely Planet moment that only comes from genuine exchanges between strangers from different cultures.

Unlike in Darwin, no one in Cambodia asked us why we weren't flying to our destination. I doubt that many of the people we saw had ever set foot on a plane. The roads were raised, cutting through a landscape of subsistence agriculture. Farms were under half a metre of rising floodwater brought on by extreme and unseasonal weather. There was no assistance for the flood-affected parts of the country. We watched from bus windows. In exercising our freedom to choose not to fly, we saw that some are more free to choose than others.

It was then I felt most strongly that the cost of flying isn't paid for with a ticket. Extreme weather, synonymous with a changing climate, is set to have the greatest impact on the least equipped and poorest people. Institutional support is often reactive, inefficient and disorganized. The people we saw combating flooding in their homes are also the lowest-per-capita emitters of greenhouse gases. The least responsible have become the worst affected. Meanwhile the more fortunate continue to fly, exhausting the capacity of the atmosphere to maintain a safe environment for all. We were acutely aware of having the means to travel to a UN climate talk through flooded towns in the developing world.

Battambang to Phnom Penh, a distance of about 290 km (180 miles), was a smooth ride. We took a tuk-tuk over to the Cambodian capital's train station to find that it had long been in disuse and was occupied by squatters. But we soon found a cheap and luxurious bus to Ho Chi Minh City – probably the most comfortable bus I've ever seen – operated by and carrying well-dressed Chinese businessmen building new economic ties with Cambodia, to feed China's expanding appetite for resources.

We crossed the border into Vietnam late at night, our fourth border crossing. Each country was separated from the next with strict controls on people's movement, but the borders felt arbitrary. The culture and language, which seemed similar from one town to the next, gradually changed as we crossed the continent. We arrived in Ho Chi Minh City for breakfast and spent the next three days enjoying the splendour that is the Vietnamese capital. We arranged to meet more climate activists, but underestimated the wall-to-wall peak-hour traffic. If only we had known about the dysfunctional transport system! Our taxi ride across town was hopeless as the streets and their pavements were gridlocked with smog-heavy scooter traffic.

On our last day in south Vietnam we boarded an overnight train to Hanoi, the beginning of an all-train journey from Ho Chi Minh City to Poznan. Vietnam to Europe on train tracks all the way. The old hand-painted posters of landscapes in the Singaporean train station hadn't prepared us for the visual feast that awaited us: the glorious Vietnamese coast, with its glimpses of steep-sided islands stepping out across the South China Sea.

We arrived in Hanoi in mid-October. In this ancient city full of myth, we enjoyed restaurants, karaoke bars and the hospitality of more activists. Unlike us, they could not afford to attend the conference. We learned what activism meant to young Vietnamese people whose freedoms were restricted in ways we had never experienced ourselves. The people we met were exceedingly brave and generous, and invited us to enjoy their finest hospitality, despite the police restrictions on what a host might provide to foreigners. The memory of their kindness still inspires me to open my home to other idealistic travellers.

At times like these, I felt most grateful for having taken the road less travelled. For many people, even short-distance travel is defined by flight. Dates, cost, duration: it all starts and ends with a flight. When someone decides to travel, limitless destinations are accessible by air. It seems empowering; after all, the mantra of the liberalized world offers us the freedom to choose as if it were a right. But what options are we really free to choose from?

Commercial travel operators, airports, airlines, hotels and car rental companies all sell the idea of an exotic journey, but there is little to nothing exotic about flying. We leave one liminal zone with a largely prescribed luggage set, only to arrive in another having learned nothing about the places between. A plane ticket can bring us so close to so much, but in contact with nothing other than the destination. Apart from odd glimpses of landscape through the clouds, what of the people below, their paths, their lives and their cultures? From the comfort of our cafe and carriage windows, we watched planes overtake us and tried to guess where they were going. I had never noticed so many planes. Halfway through our journey, we were becoming familiar and comfortable with our seemingly endless road. Thanks to our careful visa planning ahead of the trip, the journey into China was simple. We crossed thousands of rural and urban kilometres, glimpsing a cross section of the vast and booming nation. Beijing had just hosted the Olympics and was still on show, with clean streets and tall walls surrounding the older, single-level dwellings. Again, we connected with young people brought together by a passion for responsible stewardship of a global commons. Over dinner, I learned about the public expressions of young activists in an ever-sensitive China: their frustrations and their unanimous belief in China's right to develop – an important perspective in a climate debate.

After two beautiful but icy days in Beijing, we caught an early train towards Moscow. We had prepared thoroughly with food stores, books, games and clean clothes to last six days on the 7,622 km (4,736 mile) journey. We were rewarded for catching our train in the cold dawn with almost day-long views of the Great Wall.

We passed through the endless expanse of northern China and Mongolia before joining the Trans-Siberian Railway by Lake Baikal. We swapped books and watched the time zones pass by our windows. Sunset at lunchtime? Time to change my clock again. Outside the window on old roads and through snowy woods were rusting railways, factories and forgotten fields: the remnants of an extensive Russian economy. The seemingly endless chains of rail freightcars transporting oil gave only a hint of how much fuel the country needed to run today.

Our Chinese diesel train chugged on until we arrived in beautiful, serious Moscow. After two days exploring Russia's freezing capital, we boarded our final overnight train travelling through Belarus to Warsaw, Poland. We were excited about reuniting with team mates who had not been able to join the overland journey. With vodka at hand, we savoured our last night in the world of travel which had become both a challenge and a comfort.

Originally, I had set out to experience what it really feels like to reduce emissions by reducing flying. What I found differed from my expectations: I discovered that travel without flying is widely underappreciated.

Surface travel, only recently usurped by the profitable marketing of aviation, is still vitally important and realistic. Routes over land and sea have defined human history. The renaissance in the global trafficking of goods under sail, today led by fair-trade pioneers like the New Dawn Traders, will provide some solutions to the challenges of global equity and energy supply.

I also discovered that surface travel is relatively affordable when a traveller is not under a significant time constraint. I spent less than £1,500 for the privilege of a 40-day trip through 11 countries. A flight would have been much faster and slightly cheaper, but considering my experiences − street food and karaoke bars, golden sand and Pacific sky, the deep jungle, expansive plains and new friendships – that same flight would hold very little real value.

The private sector, no matter how well meaning, is incapable of regulating jet-propelled aviation in ways consistent with natural limits and equitable international development. It is hampered by legal requirements to provide a profit to shareholders. Neither will the actions of a committed few solve the global challenge of climate change: who will have access to and use of the remaining resources and atmospheric capacity? Those who promote an alternative are vital. Their sparking conversation creates the political and cultural space necessary for a sustainable future. Governments must be pushed, and it is up to all of us to do that pushing. In many of the countries I travelled through, I met people who support alternatives to flying: they are global allies in the face of steep aviation market growth.

When we finally arrived in Poznan, we were tired but jubilant. The train pulled into our last station, within sight of the UN conference centre. Young people from around the world greeted us as we alighted into the early-winter morning. The journey seemed to have ended abruptly, but really we had only just begun what promises to be a lifetime appreciation for overland travel and social and ecological tourism, and a commitment to leave no problem of resource consumption unchallenged.

Next time you travel, I invite you to consider how. It's not impossible to travel on the earth. It's not even very difficult. It is empowering, memorable and very real. I have flown since the journey described here, after much deliberation, but not frivolously as I once did. I am currently planning another surface-based trip home again to Australia from the UK. This time, I hope to overcome the sea.

Carbon Planet Auditing undertook a carbon audit of our efforts. If all five of us had flown, we would have incurred greenhouse gas emissions with a warming effect equivalent to 20.4 tonnes of carbon dioxide (tCO_2e). If we could have avoided flights altogether, by taking a boat from Darwin to Singapore, we would have produced only 9.78 tCO_2e – a reduction of 10.64 tCO_2e. As it happened, our five-person mainly overland journey resulted in an effect calculated as 12.96 tCO_2e, or less than two-thirds of the emissions produced via the same journey by air. By taking buses to Darwin, three of us managed to save 1.14 tCO_2e.

References

Committee on Climate Change (2009). 'Meeting the UK aviation target – options for reducing emissions to 2050'. Retrieved from www.theccc.org.uk/publication/meeting-the-uk-aviation-target-options-for-reducing-emissions-to-2050/

15. Travel on a hot planet: exploring the global tourist industry overland

Anirvan Chatterjee and Barnali Ghosh

Photo © Charlie Hsu

Anirvan Chatterjee is a tech geek and the founder of BookFinder.com, and **Barnali Ghosh** is a landscape architect and advocate working at the intersection of cities and climate. Their passion for sustainable transportation and deep concern about the impacts of climate change led them to spend 2009–10 doing a year-long green-citizen journalism project, Year of No Flying (www.yearofnoflying.com), writing on issues related to global transportation and climate justice as they attempted to travel around the world aviation-free. They conducted over 60 interviews with climate-justice activists, NGO workers, and climate-impacted community members at the same time travelling to 60 cities in 14 countries by cargo ship, ferry, express bus and train. They are founding members of the US-based Aviation Justice coalition (www.aviationjustice.com), formed in 2010 to raise awareness about the impacts of aviation related to climate change, noise, pollution and civil rights while advocating alternatives to an unsustainable system.

It isn't hard to lead a conventional 'green' lifestyle in Berkeley, California. We had made a conscious decision to eat mostly organic and vegetarian, and to live in a small but comfortable apartment in a somewhat dense urban community that allowed us to be car-free. With all that, we had thought that we had one of the smaller carbon footprints in the USA. But our worlds were upturned the night we used our first carbon calculator, inspired by Al Gore's documentary *An Inconvenient Truth*. We were stunned to discover that our carbon footprint that year was larger than that of 90 per cent of Americans. How could that have happened? We dug deeper into the numbers, and discovered the culprit: air travel. Like many privileged people in the First World, we had taken flying for granted, utterly unaware of its environmental impacts. We were familiar with the grey fumes coming out of auto tail-pipes, but the invisibility of plane emissions had also made it invisible to our understanding of what pollution looked like.

The second revelation was the disproportionate impact that flying has on emissions. One doesn't have to be a constant globe-trotter to start seeing aviation emissions dominate one's carbon footprint. We discovered that our annual round-trip flight to India had the same impact as an average American driving a car for a year. As a couple who prided ourselves on living car-free, we suddenly found ourselves the not-so-proud 'owners' of the climate equivalent of two cars. The handful of flights we took every year was undoing every other green effort we made.

The culture of aviation surrounds us, from our personal histories to the communities we choose to inhabit. For us, growing up in families of post-1965 transnational immigrants, our family histories are deeply connected with access to air travel – countless flights to and from India, Canada, Nigeria, Oman and the USA. Our fondest stories begin and end in airports. And all around us we are subjected to countless conversations about foreign holidays, some planned, others embarked on at the drop of a hat. Then there are the 'enlightened' travellers who feel the need to contribute in some way, especially when travelling to 'developing' countries. They fly to poorer countries to build houses with Habitat for Humanity, teach English abroad, or go off to save turtles, coming back with stories of how their lives have changed. And, indeed, there are many reasons to travel. It offers opportunities for leisure and discovery, enables us to see friends and family, expands our view of the world and allows us to escape from the everyday monotony of our modern lives. Air travel delivers novel and life-changing experiences in hours, not days, so as to fit neatly into our busy lives.

Global warming is a numbers game, so once we knew the numbers we could hum and haw, but it didn't take us long to realize that if we need to reduce carbon emissions by 90 per cent by 2050, then we can't exclude the aviation sector. This single industry is responsible for 4.9 per cent of global emissions, taking forcings and cloud formation impacts into account (Lee et al., 2009). If the aviation industry were a country, it would be one of the top ten emitters in the world.

And who are the people most affected by our aviation emissions? Not us, but the people of Haiti, Bangladesh, Sierra Leone, Zimbabwe and Madagascar (the five most climate-vulnerable nations in the world according to Maplecroft, 2012). Every time the world's frequent flyers step on a plane, a distant part of the planet suffers. Every time we got on a plane, we were harming someone. Yet, at home in the USA, the reality of climate change was nearly invisible in the media, and even green organizations weren't talking about the disproportionate impact that flying had on the environment.

We wanted to see for ourselves what these climate impacts looked like, and what climate action looked like around the world. But we couldn't bring ourselves to make the journeys by plane, knowing everything we knew, so we had to improvise.

Nine months later, we found ourselves on a container ship in the middle of the Pacific Ocean. It would be the start of a year spent hearing from local environmental activists, researchers and policy analysts about the real impacts that climate change was having on local lives and livelihoods, and the ways in which communities were adapting. We captured the stories in text and photos, bringing them back to our communities and cross-fertilising ideas between activists in different regions. Our personal challenge was to try to do all this without flying, aiming to understand first-hand what it might mean to live in a carbon-constrained world where global elites like us could no longer take aviation for granted. Our 'year of no flying' might turn out to be a failure, but at a time of impending ecological crisis, we felt moved to explore these questions.

We set out to experience a world without flying. This inherently meant experiencing a slower pace of travel, discovering new modes of transport, and being open to unfamiliar experiences. The first step of our journey took us across the Pacific Ocean by container ship from Seattle to Tokyo.

This is an excerpt from our Year of No Flying blog, trying to describe ten days at sea:

> **PACIFIC OCEAN:** Though we fall into a routine, the rocking of the boat and the view from the window of the freighter, with its colourful containers making their way boldly to an ever-moving horizon, is a constant reminder that we are in the middle of the Pacific with no land in sight. The oceans grow worse-tempered come fall. Our

activity during the days and nights is intertwined with the ocean's moods. We sit outside, play ping-pong, read, write, and eat full meals when the waves are gentle. And on those other days when the ship has no other choice but to bend to the swell of the ocean and the force of the gales, we struggle to stay awake, force ourselves to eat a bit so as to not be nauseated, distract ourselves with movies to escape the rattling of the doors, and lie malleably in bed, letting the ocean rock us to sleep… And in ten days there is that one perfect day. The sea is content just lapping up gently against the ship, as if they are friends again. As if that fight that we had watched between them that other night was just another trivial event – the ocean had forgotten that it was feeling just a little bit taken advantage of, and instead was enjoying the company of its friend who had come to visit. A gentle and warm breeze blows. Geography has been navigated and we are in warmer climes. Sunlight skims the top of the water depending on the mood of the clouds that hang in the sky – billowy and huge. The cup of tea, the sound of inspired fingers tapping at the keyboard, the presence of a loved one in one's peripheral vision and then that slightly imperfect smell of exhaust make this a perfect moment.

It is this first journey by container ship that tends to capture the imagination of most people who hear our story. Not flying can be a worthwhile endeavour in itself. Like slow food, slow travel gives us a greater appreciation of time and distance, of boundaries and of sense of place. Train travel is the most common form of slow travel. It may have been receding into the realm of nostalgia in the USA, but train travel was alive and well in Asia, not yet completely replaced by cheap flights.

JAPAN: We discovered high-speed train travel in Japan with the Shinkansen, running at speeds of 300 km/hr (190 mph). You could set your clock by the departure time, and the frequency of the trains allowed us to book our tickets the same day or the day before. The best part was the lack of security checks; we took the local metro to the train station, arriving ten minutes before the train departure time. Trains and bathrooms were always clean, courtesy of the ladies in pink. Train seats were able to be rotated to face the direction of travel – great for avoiding motion sickness. Each seat had a little map of the train showing the nearest exits, bathrooms, and so on. We loved these small design details. Kyoto to Hiroshima in two hours! Only one complaint: with high-speed train travel, getting to your destination is so quick, there's really no time to explore train food.

SHANGHAI: While in Shanghai, we took a 40 yuan (£4) joyride on a train pitched as the fastest you can go without flying: 431 km/hr (268 mph). The maglev journey took us from the city to the airport, the first of a planned series of high-speed rail lines around China. Electronic displays inside the train showed the current speed; the whole car buzzed with excitement as we hit the maximum speed. We covered the distance in a swift eight minutes, so fast that we didn't get a sense of what was happening. … High-speed rail is amazing; at these speeds, Bangalore to Kolkata would take about four and a half hours, and San Francisco to Los Angeles could be covered in about one and a half hours.

INDIA: Tangy curd rice and the reddest hottest mango pickle, wrapped in banana leaf: heaven! We never failed to pick up this treat from Vijaywada, a small station somewhere between Madras and Calcutta. The curd and rice were rumoured to be set together, giving it its unique taste. Oranges in Nagpur, biryani in some station in Kerala, milky tea in mud pots in Kolkata – every station had its unique culinary delights: watery rasam, spicy sambhar, rice and puris, potato curry, curd and pickles. Train meals were simple but satisfying, one of the best parts of the trip. If you were lucky, your fellow passengers would share the food they had brought with them from home, usually dry, spicy treats, built to last the journey. ...

VIETNAM: Train journeys never had a soundtrack before. But in Vietnam, the music was everywhere. We watched children, farmers, dragons, ducks and water buffalos dance, skip and play on the water puppet stage in Hanoi. The music was high-pitched, rhythmic and haunting, and it followed us everywhere. In cities, it was soft, but when we boarded the train and passed by green rice fields with water buffalos, egrets and ducks, it became so loud that it over-whelmed our emotions in a most pleasurable way. The Vietnamese countryside is stunning, and it glistens in the rain. I had heard that it was particularly breathtaking between Hue and Danang; our train hugged the coast and ascended the mountain. Waves thrashed on one side and the green mountains rose on the other. We couldn't decide which way to look, but one never knows what the window will frame.

NANNING, CHINA: We saw our favourite view out the window near Nanning, China. As the train proceeded, we suddenly found ourselves in a magical land-scape. The sun was setting and in that orange glow, lime-stone karst formations rose near and far. The karst forms themselves seemed mythical, changing into silhouettes. The sun set slowly and we took many deep breaths, in dis-belief that we were watching this wondrous view from our humble train car. Sights like this are what train journeys are made of and the experiences and memories of which wash away those other minor inconveniences.

We would have the opportunity to take many more trains. The grandest of these journeys would be aboard the trains of the Trans-Siberian. We rode China's newest high-speed trains – clean and comfortable. In Russia, we took clean, compact and organized trains from Moscow to St Petersburg and then from Moscow to Odessa in Ukraine. In Turkey we rode a train that was so comfortable and stylish that we regretted that it was only an eight-hour journey. Taking trains in Europe, including the Eurostar from Paris to London, seemed the normal and obvious way to travel. Yet we dreaded having to take Amtrak across the USA. To our surprise, we were delighted by the experience of crossing the country aboard the *California Zephyr*. These rail tracks, built by Chinese immigrant labourers, brought us face to face with the USA's most stunning landscapes. But disinvestment in the system and the prioritisation of freight over passenger trains had resulted in a system that was unreliable and disreputable.

Container-ship stories speak of adventure, trains of nostalgia, but the lowly bus evokes no such commendation. Yet buses are the most reliable low-carbon option for travel. Middle-class Americans tend to turn up their noses at the Greyhound buses that cross the country. In most Asian countries, we found long-distance buses were often death traps, with drivers regularly tempting fate as they jumped across lanes, playing chicken with their compatriots coming in the other direction. It was in Turkey we discovered the true potential of bus travel: stunning, well-kept stations and rest stops, a well-connected bus network, comfortable seats and, on some buses, service with tea, biscuits and water. Best of all, it was the way all the locals travelled. Half a year later, on our return to the East Coast of the USA, we discovered a newer breed of buses – comfortable, cheap, Wi-Fi enabled. Alas, the West Coast's lower population density had not been conducive to developing such bus lines.

Our year-long journey was carried out using one car, two container ships, three ferries, sixteen buses, thirty-nine trains and, to our dismay, two planes. We flew. From Bangkok, Thailand, to Kolkata, India. And then back again from Bangalore, India, to Shanghai, China. We'd come from California to Thailand by car, container ship, train, ferry and bus. And then we were stuck. We had no way of getting from Thailand to South Asia to see family in India, and to try to learn about the real impacts of climate change in Bangladesh. It was infuriating to be so close and yet unable to get there by land or sea. Even as we were planning our trip, we'd known that this segment was a bit of an unknown, but we'd figured we'd find a route on the road. But none of the options panned out: the sea route closed off due to security restrictions, the land route through Myanmar unavailable for Americans, the train route through Tibet and Nepal unavailable in winter. We had a choice: we could either skip South Asia and keep going, or we could take a plane flight to see our family. In the end, we picked family. Anirvan's grandfather was 93 years old; we couldn't bring ourselves to lose a chance to see him, even if it meant failing our self-imposed test. George Monbiot, the British environmental journalist, calls these 'love miles': the planet-killing air travel we do to see the ones we love. In failing to find a flight-free route from Southeast Asia to South Asia, we also discovered how pervasive aviation-oriented development can be, a hidden transport-mode monoculture.

Of course, its impact on climate isn't the only problem with aviation. Aviation-oriented development is promoted as being a great boon for communities, but it has a wide range of negative impacts. These range from aviation noise (a significant public health concern, and at the time of writing, the target of widespread protests throughout Germany) to the physical displacement of airport neighbours (Stewart et al. (2011)). As we made our way through India, we discovered how the expansion of the Chhatrapati Shivaji International Airport in Mumbai will displace massive numbers of people – at least 85,000 people will need to relocate from their homes. In India, planes transport the upper class, while dislocating those who will never see the inside of a plane. Meanwhile, the new airport in Navi Mumbai, Mumbai's twin city, will not only destroy 17 villages, but will also devastate 170 hectares (420 acres) of fast-shrinking wetlands – the region's natural defence against flooding, erosion and sea-level rise. In the developed world, much of the damage has already been done, but it's heartbreaking to see developing nations following our lead, destroying communities and natural resources to facilitate an activity that significantly contributes to global climate change.

As we travelled, we found ourselves constantly questioning the contradictions of travel. It certainly made us more aware, opening us to different ways of seeing the world. And we can't deny that we enjoyed almost every minute of it. But at what cost? We're told by aviation boosters that people won't want to save fragile places until they see them for themselves, and yet the reality of climate change means that the very act of flying somewhere to see it can help ruin it. The more you see, the less there is to see.

During our trip, we often got advice like 'Don't bother going there' or 'Go there, it hasn't been discovered yet'. Travel, it seemed, was all about avoiding tourists. Traveller tips that wrote off entire nations were particularly depressing; tourists just like us had used and abused these places, chewing them up and then spitting them out. Pioneering international travellers may have had a lighter footprint (when they weren't wearing the boots of colonialism), but in being unable to keep their 'discoveries' a secret, they opened the door for mass-market tourism, and for the creation of cringeworthy places like Khao San Road in Bangkok and the beaches of Sihanoukville in Cambodia. Places like these seemed to have emerged out of a vacuum, utterly unrelated to the spaces around them, targeting a certain kind of tourist who wants to be hundreds of miles away from home, and yet be the same person (but more cheaply and with less supervision).

It wasn't until we spoke with Bangkok-based tourism researcher Anita Pleumarom that we began to understand the full extent of the problems that tourism creates. Her work with the Tourism Investigation and Monitoring Team (TIM-TEAM) focuses on the failure of tourism-oriented development in developing nations, which she describes as 'sheer economic exploitation', with most of the money going to multinational corporations (for example, airlines, tour operators and hotels) and only a pittance trickling down to local communities. Pleumarom and her allies around the world are engaged in both local community planning debates and international campaigns like fighting for civil society participation in the UN World Tourism Agency. As well-meaning liberals from the rich world, we've seen a plethora of advertising for ecotourism and cultural tourism products targeting our demographic. Pleumarom took us behind the scenes, telling us about communities forced to continuously 'stage authenticity' for outsiders, mass-scale home stays becoming an immense intrusion on locals' privacy, and tour operators creating sex and drug trades by providing women and opium to tourists. She argues that tourism can be a self-destructive force – the initial wave of benefits from new tourism ends as mass operators move into the market, community economic benefits decrease, and the destination finally becomes 'too touristy', leading travellers to look elsewhere for new 'undiscovered' spots.

We were struck by the role of aviation in this process. Airlines are among the biggest beneficiaries of overseas travel of all categories, including 'responsible' tourism, 'eco' tourism and 'voluntourism'.

'Air travel is an elitist activity,' Anita Pleumarom explained, enjoyed by only a few per cent of the world's inhabitants. 'At the end of the day, it's about an equal distribution of resources, including the atmosphere… Aviation and tourism don't reflect the real price, which includes exploitation of Third World communities.' And perhaps that means that 'the industry needs to shrink'. Pleumarom has been working to limit her own personal air travel, including cancelling her frequent-flyer miles, but quickly points out that 'as individual consumers, we can't do much – we need to change the system'. This certainly requires sustainable transportation options, but reducing unsustainable discretionary travel will also mean changing the way we feel about our jobs, our lives and our communities; addressing what it is that makes residents of developed nations so often feel they desperately need to escape their everyday lives to visit overseas holiday resorts.

Over the course of our journey, we spent a lot of time thinking about what a world with less unsustainable aviation would look like; it almost invariably seems to mean less travel, less tourism, less contact with the wider world – the very experiences that we were enjoying on the road. Though Anita Pleumarom was far too polite to bring it up, aviation is a small part of a larger system, and we can't pretend that we're not implicated, even if we choose to travel without flying. Travel has enormous power to shape our views about the world, but in the face of catastrophic global climate change, we all need to think more deeply before jumping on a plane, even if we can afford it. And perhaps more of us will stay closer to home when we need that break, go deeper into the places where we live, and learn to develop love and empathy for places and people without needing to go there.

Our flight-free trip was inspired in large part by work being done in the UK. The British environmental action and policy community have managed to generate substantial public discussion about the massive climate impacts of aviation, to the point where it's a matter of mainstream political and ethical debate. We wanted to know more. But then something amazing happened right before we arrived in London: against all odds, British environmentalists won the 'Battle of Heathrow'.

We spent our time in the UK interviewing participants in the decade-long struggle to prevent an expansion of Heathrow airport, the most visible battlefield against an industry spewing 13 per cent of British greenhouse gas emissions (Aviation Environment Federation, 2007). Campaign organizers brought together affected Heathrow neighbours, environmental direct action activists and fiscal conservatives in a remarkable coalition that managed to hold together against a heavy political and public-relations assault. When a new Conservative-led government was elected in 2010, one of its first moves was to shut down Heathrow's expansion. We've written the full story of the Heathrow campaign on our Year of No Flying blog, and the organizer, John Stewart, has also written an excellent tactical history of the battle against the third runway (Stewart, n.d.).

We returned to the USA deeply inspired by this movement that had challenged the seemingly unchecked growth of aviation pollution.

Since our return, we have continued to work on the issue of aviation and the environment, informed by what we learned during our trip. We started off looking only at global climate concerns, but we learned in London that local and global go together. Upon our return, we found new allies among airport neighbours fighting local aviation noise and pollution impacts. In New York, Chicago, Los Angeles and Seattle, community organizers were busy fighting to defend their communities against Big Aviation – and they were delighted to be able to add the climate argument to their arsenal. Together, we formed the Aviation Justice coalition, working towards a more just aviation industry and advocating alternatives to an unsustainable system. In 2011 we organized a national tour for British anti-aviation activists John Stewart and Dan Glass, inspiring audiences in seven cities with the first-hand story of their victory at Heathrow. (We were hoping to have Stewart and Glass appear in person, but when US immigration prevented their entry, we fell back to a greener solution, organizing a national speaking tour entirely via videoconferencing.)

The facts are clear. Flying is responsible for about 5 per cent of human impact on the climate, and at current rates sectoral emissions will quadruple by 2050 (Lee et al., 2009). But in spite of this, flying remains an elite activity: roughly 95 per cent of the people on the planet have never flown (Sachs, 2002). It's ironic that so many people in the rich world complain about the cost of aviation, even as those costs entirely omit the massive hidden environmental and social costs. Until those costs are reflected, it's up to all of us to acknowledge the hidden costs, to keep pushing forward so that future generations might live in a world beyond dirty aviation, where they can uniformly enjoy the efficiency of high-speed rail, the decadence of slow travel, the connectedness of ubiquitous videoconferencing, and the knowledge of having created fewer climate refugees. Our year of no flying was a glimpse into that other world.

References

Aviation Environment Federation (2007). 'It's 13% – official!' Retrieved from www.aef.org.uk/?p=109

Lee, D. S. et al. (2009). 'Aviation and global climate change in the 21st century'. *Atmospheric Environment*, 43 (22–23): 3520–37.

Maplecroft (2012). 'World's fastest growing populations increasingly vulnerable to the impacts of climate change – 4th global atlas reports' (press release). Retrieved from http://maplecroft.com/about/news/ccvi_2012.html

Sachs, W. (2002). 'Globalization and sustainability.' In B. Harriss-White (ed.), *Globalization and Insecurity*. Basingstoke: Palgrave.

Stewart, J. (n.d.). 'Victory against all the odds'. Retrieved from http://hacan.org.uk/resources/reports/victory.pdf

Stewart, J., McManus, F., Rodgers, N., Weedon, V., and Bronzaft, A. (2011). *Why noise matters: A worldwide perspective on the problems, policies and solutions*. Abingdon: Routledge.

How to fly less

If you are among the 1 per cent of humanity who fly and you wish to fly less, then you may find these travel tips useful.

1 Measure the CO_2 emissions that you were responsible for last year. Using carbon calculators will get your aviation emissions in perspective with your other emissions. Get to know approximate emissions for transport options on your regular journeys. Some useful carbon calculator websites include www.ecopassenger.com, carboncalculator.direct.gov.uk and www.carbonzero.co.nz

2 Tell your family, friends and colleagues why you fly less.

3 Become a seasoned traveller by sustainable transport. Get to know timetables, routes, fares, facilities and services offered by train and bus operators. www.Seat61.com is an excellent place to start. Within Europe www.loco2.com offers cross-border rail bookings and www.eurolines.com offers bus travel information.

4 Take satisfaction in knowing that you are encouraging more sustainable transport businesses by purchasing long-distance bus and train tickets.

5 Use time on sustainable transport. Most sustainable transport journeys over 300 km (190 miles) take longer than flying, but this extra time can be used productively for working, sleeping, reading or whatever you enjoy.

6 When you do travel, make the most of being away. For example, consider taking your holiday after a business conference so you create only one journey's worth of pollution.

7 If you take any flights, navigate the most carbon-efficient routes and use the most fuel-efficient aircraft per passenger. Favour direct flights on the most fuel-efficient aircraft with airlines achieving the maximum load factors. Use trains or buses on sections of the journey where you can.

8 Use sustainable freight transport methods. Cargo ships and trains are very fuel-efficient for long-distance freight.

9 Live where you work, so you can avoid commuting by air.

10 If you buy a holiday home, choose one that you will access by car or train.

11 Find alternatives to flying for work. Avoid those early 'red-eye' departures, the indignity of airport security, officious instructions and getting home late.

12 Use videoconferencing. As authors in this book have shown, videoconferencing can be a great alternative to travel – cheaper, easier and much less carbon intensive.

13 Don't bother to 'offset' carbon from your flights. The climate change from each flight will induce more climate change before 'offsetting' is effective. See www.cheatneutral.com for more information on offsetting.

Index

The Power of Just Doing Stuff
How local action can change the world
197 x 128 mm, 160pp

Something is stirring. People around the world are deciding that the well-being of their community and its economy lies with them. They're people like you. They've had enough, and, rather than waiting for permission, they're rolling up their sleeves, getting together with friends and neighbours, and doing something about it. Whether they start small or big, they're finding that just doing stuff can transform their neighbourhoods and their lives. *The Power of Just Doing Stuff* argues that this shift represents the seeds of a new economy – the answer to our desperate search for a new way forward – and at its heart is people deciding that change starts with them. Communities worldwide are already modelling a more local economy rooted in place, in well-being, in entrepreneurship, and in creativity.

> "Rob Hopkins has done more to change the way that we live in the past 10 years than anyone else in Britain. Because he has given people the tools to create change for themselves. It is beautifully simple and incredibly powerful."
> **Monty Don, gardener, writer and broadcaster**

Changeology
How to enable groups, communities and societies to do things they've never done before

234 x 156 mm, 272pp

Changeology is about influencing the behaviour of human beings for the better. The pressing issues of today such as climate change, poverty, obesity, AIDS and drug use clamour for solutions, yet, to a surprising degree, past and present efforts to effect social change have been based on little more than hunches. This book dispels many of the myths that prevent social change projects from succeeding, and replaces them with the best of what we know from social and motivational psychology and lessons from projects that have worked.

"A beguilingly simple framework for effective social change illustrated with loads of helpful and inspiring examples. Thought provoking at every turn, I finished the book buzzing with new ideas to try out in my own work."
Nigel Topping, Chief Innovation Officer, Carbon Disclosure Project

The Nature of Business
Redesigning for resilience

234 x 156 mm, 272pp

Going beyond current approaches to responsible and green business, Hutchins focuses on the emergence of new ways of operating and creating value in an increasingly volatile and interconnected world. He makes the compelling case that the 'Firm of the Future' should seek to mimic behaviours and organisations found in nature, which offer fitting models for businesses capable of flourishing in chaotic and uncertain times. A 'Firm of the Future', he argues, builds resilience, optimises, adapts, integrates systems, navigates by values and supports life-building activities. It is a business inspired by nature.

"A must-read for everyone involved in the business of the future ... and aren't we all?"
Mick Bremans, Chairman, Ecover

About Green Books

Green Books has been publishing books on environmental and ecological issues for more than 21 years. We were winners in the Environmental category at both the 2009 British Book Design and Production Awards and the 2010 Independent Publishing Awards.

Join our mailing list:

Find out about forthcoming titles, new editions, special offers, reviews, author appearances, events, interviews, podcasts, etc.
www.greenbooks.co.uk/subscribe

How to order:

Get details of stockists and online bookstores. (Remember that you can also order direct from our website.) If you are a bookstore, find out about our distributors or contact us to discuss your particular requirements.
www.greenbooks.co.uk/order

Send us a book proposal:

If you want to write – even if you have just the kernel of an idea at present – we'd love to hear from you. We pride ourselves on supporting our authors and making the process of book-writing as satisfying and as easy as possible.
www.greenbooks.co.uk/for-authors